explorations in Christian belief

by Lisa M Clark and Donald Macaskill

PARISH EDUCATION PUBLICATIONS

First published in Great Britain
in 2000 by Parish Education Publications
Annie Small House
18 Inverleith Terrace
Edinburgh EH3 5NS

ISBN 0-86153-294-5

Cover and interior design by Heather Macpherson
Typeset by Heather Macpherson
Line drawings by Lesley Moncrieff

Printed and bound in the UK by Image & Print Group

Contents

Introduction

Explorations in Christian belief

This book is about questions.

Questions are part and parcel of what it means to be human. Yet at some times and when faced with certain issues questions are felt to be inappropriate. For instance, when it comes to Christianity, many people feel that matters of belief should just be accepted – and no questions asked. This book seeks to challenge that assumption by asking you the reader to come prepared to ask about, and reflect on, some of the questions which relate to believing or not believing as Christians at the start of a new millennium.

The material

The text is based on material which has been used with small groups around Scotland, and which has been adapted and developed for a wider audience. It is intended that the material will suit both existing and new groups; study groups and housegroups as well as those who would like to use the material for communicants' classes and enquirers' groups.

The units do not seek to give answers, but to provoke debate and reflection on some of the fundamental issues affecting what Christians do and do not believe in, and to reflect the diversity of the Christian tradition.

It is anticipated that those who use this book will be involved in a struggle. A struggle to understand the nature of God and of Christ; to reflect on what prayer is; to consider what the worship and sacraments of the Church are all about; to relate believing to belonging to a religious community and a wider society; to think about how we use the Bible; to meditate generally on the implications of seeking to be Christian today. Struggling is at the heart of faith, and is often the means by which we come to know God in a more profound way. But so, too, is enjoyment. The authors hope that those who choose to read and use these studies will enjoy the task, and will find that their faith is deepened, opened up, and challenged along the way.

How to use the book

Each unit deals with a distinct issue, and would normally take up one evening's work. It may be, however, that you feel some of the units deserve more time within your particular group: it is up to you to decide. Each unit offers introductory text and exercises, some of which are based on reading and responding, some asking you to look at and reflect on pictures or illustrations.

It is our belief that this material is best explored in small groups of no more than 7-8 people.

Though it is possible to get the best out of it with even fewer people than this, we suggest if you have a larger number embarking on this material, that you divide into smaller groups – perhaps occasionally meeting up also to exchange results. This is not least because the sharing of answers and reflecting on one another's responses plays a big part in the way this material has been used and developed; in smaller groups it tends to be easier to ensure that all participants will respond fully. The units have been written in a way which means it is possible for copies of the book to be shared by a number of people, although it would certainly be easier if each group member had their own copy of the study.

You will find that some of the units refer on to a section entitled 'Further Reading' where the topic receives more coverage. These sections provide a more detailed level of explanation, and are for those who would like to do a little more in-depth reading on a particular subject. Don't be put off by them, they are quite optional: you can opt to skip these pages, or use them to explore the topic further.

Finally, what is contained in this book is not the last word - even for the two authors. It is a start: the rest, as they say, is up to you. The views and opinions expressed here are meant to challenge: and just occasionally, you can spot a rogue devil's advocate lurking between the lines.

Enjoy! - and re-discover faith.

Revd Dr Donald Macaskill is the Vice-Principal of the Scottish Churches Open College as well as Secretary for the Readership within the Church of Scotland. He has been involved in Christian adult education for more than ten years.

Lisa Clark is the National Adviser in Adult Christian Education for the Church of Scotland's Board of Parish Education. Lisa has extensive experience of leading adult learning groups throughout Scotland and has initiated a number of key new projects within the Church of Scotland.

GOD

In this section, we will consider and spend some time thinking about God. How God is described in the Hebrew Scriptures which we know as the Old Testament; reflecting on the way in which the Jewish people changed and developed their understanding of God. We shall examine the influence of the life and death of Jesus and the effect it had on altering ideas about God. But first of all we shall start by thinking of what God means to us.

On your own think about a

- *person*
- *place*
- *song*

that has spoken to you of God.

Then share your thoughts with a neighbour.

When you think about God, what picture do you have? Has this picture changed from when you were a child?

Look at the pictures on ***page 85****.*

- *Which one do you respond to most?*
- *Can you describe what it says to you?*
- *Are there any of these pictures which leave you feeling cold, which do not speak to you of God?*
- *Can you give some reasons why this might be?*

Share your answers with someone in the group or in the larger group.

The reason we have so many pictures of God even within a group of people is because there are many influences which have helped to shape the way in which we understand God. It is important that we take time to recognise what these have been and that they will inevitably be different for different people.

What do *you* think have been the most important influences in shaping your picture of God? These might include a bible story or stories; people you have met; experiences you have had; things you have heard in church or a book you have read?

Our understanding of God is made up of and affected by things which have happened and are still happening to us in our lives. The kind of relationship we have with God is personal and is therefore affected by all that has made us who we are.

Many of the words and pictures which we use to describe God come to us from the Bible. There we find the story of individuals and communities as they struggled to know and understand God, and what was happening in their lives.

We will now look at some of the ways in which God has been understood in the Old and New Testaments and see how these have influenced us.

Understanding of God in the Old Testament

The Hebrew Scriptures, which we know as the Old Testament, give us an unfolding idea of God from the point of view of a particular people, across eight hundred years of their history. They include the insights given to inspired individuals and give a picture of God always seen in relationship to a people and their political and cultural development. They show influences from Israel's earlier history and relationship with the beliefs of different peoples. You might find the Further Reading section useful at this point, see **page 144**.

The reason we look at the Old Testament in some depth is that it provides the foundation for many of our views of God.

Divide the following passages amongst groups of those present.

- *Look at the passage.*
- *Think of the words used to describe how God appears in these texts.*
- *Then say whether the group was comfortable or uncomfortable with this image.*
- *Has this image affected at all the way in which **you** view God?*

Genesis 3:8	God walking in the garden
Genesis 6:5-8	God the annihilator (with some favourites)
Exodus 14:24-31	God of Israel!
Exodus 22:17-28	The moral God
1 Kings 18:20-40	God of blood and fire
1 Kings 19:9-18	God of noise, silence and death
Psalm 21:7-13	The destroying God
Psalm 139:1-6	The comforting God
Job 37:20-24	The awesome God
Isaiah 55:1-3	The providing God

Are there other stories in the Old Testament which have not been mentioned, but which help in your understanding of God?

Understanding of God in the New Testament

Surprisingly, there is little in the New Testament which speaks directly of God.

Christians find that the main way in which to gain an understanding of God is through the person of Jesus Christ and his life, ministry, death and resurrection. Our picture of God is developed by what Christ did and said which is recorded in the New Testament.

The New Testament also provides evidence of a significant change in the way in which people understood and spoke about God. Partly this is because of the belief that God had become a human being in the person of Jesus and therefore was able to identify and empathise with humanity in an entirely new way. It was also because belief in God was expressed in new terms which increasingly owed more to the cultures of Greece and Rome than to traditional Jewish understanding.

- *How important to you is the knowledge that God became human in the form of Jesus?*
- *In what ways does this help you to understand God better?*

Share your answers and the reasons for them, with one another.

One of the difficulties many people have is in making the link between the God they read about and discover in the Old Testament, and the God who is identified in Jesus and of whom Jesus speaks. By using a Bible which contains the Old Testament and the New Testament writings, we are affirming that this is the one and the same God. We must always be careful that we do not limit either the descriptions of God in the Old Testament by presenting a false picture of judgement, wrath and vengeance, or in the New Testament by portraying Jesus' humanity at the expense of his divinity.

A further question concerns the relationship between God the Father, Jesus the Son and the Holy Spirit. Christian theology has always struggled with how Jesus understood his relationship to God and indeed the way in which the Holy Spirit relates to God the Creator and Jesus. The Church sought to express how Jesus was at one and the same time both fully human and fully divine. It was in this context that the idea of the Trinity was developed in the early Church, using the language and ideas of the time to express the relationship between the three.

Look at Matthew 3:13-17.

- *How does it portray the relationship between Jesus and God and the Holy Spirit?*
- *How do you make sense of this relationship?*

We will look at this relationship in more detail in the unit on *The Holy Spirit.*

Understanding of God after the New Testament

Two thousand years have passed since the New Testament writers described God in relation to Jesus. In that time, our understanding of God, the way in which we think of God, has not stood still. Across the centuries people have continued to struggle with what God means to them and how they understand the divine.

Concepts of God are always influenced by what is happening in the society and time in which people live. They are affected by the ways in which people think and the culture of the age. Many of the hymns which we sing in churches today come to us from the Victorian period which had a particular view of God and the role of the Church in society. Many individuals today find the image of God contained in these hymns an uncomfortable one.

Read this hymn and describe to one another the image of God which it reflects:

God the Omnipotent! King, who ordainest
Great winds thy clarions, lightnings thy sword:
Show forth thy pity on high where thou reignest;
Give to us peace in our time, O Lord.
...

God, the All-righteous One! Man hath defied thee;
Yet to eternity standeth thy word;
Falsehood and wrong shall not tarry beside thee;
Give to us peace in our time, O Lord.
...

So shall thy children, with thankful devotion,
Praise him who saves them from peril and sword,
Singing in chorus, from ocean to ocean,
Peace to the nations, and praise to the Lord.

The *Church Hymnary* (3rd Edition), No. 516
Henry Fothergill Chorley, 1808-72 and John Ellerton 1826-93

The characteristics of God most strongly emphasised in a culture are often those which are most helpful at that particular point in history. For example, the idea of God as liberator and friend of the oppressed is very common in Latin America today. The idea of God as the one who offers eternal life was a very significant image in the Negro spirituals, most of which were composed by slaves. A look at the hymns and prayers of a people is often a good way into understanding their concept of God.

Many of the surveys carried out in Britain today show that the majority of people profess a belief in God.

- *How do you think God is understood in today's society?*

There have been many challenges to belief in God and to the picture of God as all-knowing, all-powerful and unchangeable.

- *To what extent do you think this picture of God is valid today?*

You might want to look at the Further Reading section to help you with this question.

Words for God

As we saw in looking at the Victorian hymn, the words we use provide an insight into the understanding of God held by a society or individual.

Share with one another the words you think of when you imagine God.

- *Think of the titles which are used to describe God i.e. Majesty, Creator, Father. How helpful are these words? Do they reflect the understanding of God you have spoken of? Do you think your understanding of God is shaped in part by these titles?*
- *What is your reaction to the following prayer? Do you think we should use more female images of God?*

God our mother
You nurture and love us.
You are the one,
who through the pain of birth
lets us, your children, come to life.
We love you.

God our Mother,
You are with us,
from our first steps to our last.
You give us freedom to fail.
But you never let us go.
We love you.

God our Mother,
You push us out
and challenge us.
You pull us towards adventure.
But we know we always nestle
in your loving arms.
We love you.

(Clark / Macaskill)

Look at the following cartoons. Reflecting on all you have done and thought about in this section, how do you react to the following cartoons? Do they describe your relationship with God? For each of the pictures it might appear obvious which of the characters is God - but sometimes these roles are reversed.

Share with others when you feel this to be true.

JESUS

In this section, we will consider the character of Jesus as he is described in the New Testament, and the nature of his life and ministry. We will also reflect on the way in which Jesus has been understood by the church and in contemporary society. As part of this we shall examine our understanding of Jesus' relationship to God and the events of the cross and tomb.

- *Do you have a favourite story about Jesus? Share this with one another.*
- *Why did you choose this story?*
- *What does it show about the nature of Jesus?*

Before looking at the textual evidence on Jesus, list what characteristics you think are commonly associated with him.

Now examine the following passages. What do they show about Jesus' character?

Luke 9:28-36

Luke 12:49-53

Matthew 12:46-50

John 11:33-35

Mark 11:15-17

Mark 16:19

Acts 9:3-8

Is there a difference between your first and second list?
Why do you think this might be?

Which of the following sentences do you agree/disagree with? Give each question a score as follows:

Strongly Agree (4) | Agree (3) | Disagree (2) | Strongly disagree (1)

- Jesus gives us a clear picture of what God is like.
- If there were conclusive proof discovered tomorrow that Jesus' body had been found, my faith would be severely affected.
- Jesus was a great moral teacher, in the same way that other people such as Martin Luther King or Gandhi have been in this century.
- If there were no Jesus my relationship with God would be very different.
- If we knew that Jesus had married, then he couldn't have been the Messiah.
- Jesus lived an absolutely perfect life even as a child.

For each of these sentences talk either to a person who scored close to the answer you have given; or find a person who scored very differently.

Share with them why you answered in the way that you did.

Who do you say that I am?

It would be difficult to write a full biography of Jesus from the details we have about him in the pages of the New Testament. His active ministry lasted only some three and a half years. We therefore know virtually nothing about his childhood other than one instance of a visit to the Temple in Jerusalem with his parents - where his behaviour wasn't exactly angelic! The so-called 'quest for the historical Jesus' has been a long search.

What we know of his ministry comes to us from the words of his followers years after his death, and underlines their conviction that after his crucifixion he had risen from the dead. In seeking to discover what Jesus was like we have to examine the New Testament stories about him alongside what the later writers in the early Church wrote and believed.

Even the first disciples struggled with their own understanding of who Jesus was, for them. In a famous incident Jesus asks his followers 'Who do you say that I am?' - they give a variety of different answers. From earliest times then, people struggled with terms for Christ and used different words and images to describe him in trying to answer the question of Jesus' identity.

We will look at the titles and terminology given to Jesus, both in the Gospels and in the early Church, to see the ways in which people have historically responded to the question. However, we will also note that the same title can mean and has meant different things to different people at various points in history. All of these titles point not only to who we think Jesus is, but also to how we understand Jesus' relationship with God. This will help us to begin to answer Jesus' question for ourselves and understand our own relationship with him. For each of these sections you will find further notes and explanations in the Further Reading section.

Jesus the Saviour

At its simplest level a saviour is someone who saves.

For a long period of their history the Jews looked forward to the time when someone would come and rescue them from the difficulties and distresses they were facing. They looked forward to a 'saviour' - someone who would save them, rescue them, bring them back to the good times in their relationship with God. The term 'saviour' began to develop political overtones, associated with a mighty ruler or warrior. So the idea of looking for a saviour is one which is rooted in Jewish culture and understanding. The first disciples would therefore have been very familiar with this sort of language and many of the ideas which it conveyed.

However, the early Christians began to give the word 'saviour' its own distinctive meaning which was much more individual and personal and far less political than the Jewish understanding had been.

In small groups, look at the following verses from Matthew.

> What do you think? If a shepherd has a hundred sheep, and one of them has gone astray, does he not leave the ninety-nine on the mountains and go in search of the one that went astray? And if he finds it, truly I tell you, he rejoices over it more than over the ninety-nine that never went astray. So it is not the will of your Father in heaven that one of these little ones should be lost.
>
> Matthew 18:12-14.

- *What is your initial reaction to this parable?*
- *From it, can we conclude that Jesus is a saviour?*
- *Does the story work for you as a good pattern for how Jesus should be acting as saviour?*

A saviour is someone who brings salvation, a word which Christians use a great deal. But what do we mean by the term salvation? And salvation from what?

For Jesus' original followers salvation meant saving them from sin and death. Christians affirmed their belief that Jesus too has a saving role for us, and therefore was God. This is evident in the early usage of the fish as a symbol for Christians. *Ichthus* means fish; but the letters also are an acronym for the Greek words for Jesus Christ, Son of God, Saviour.

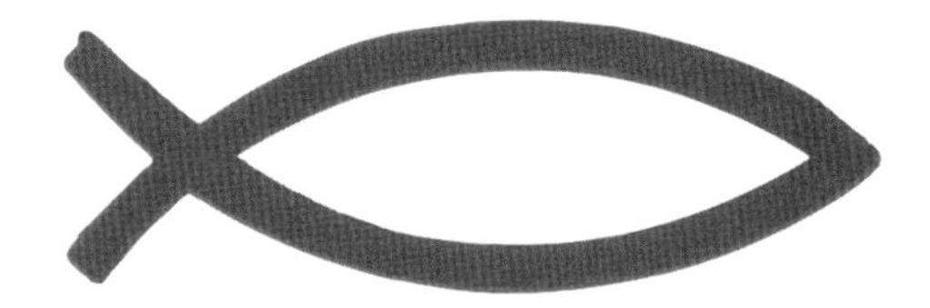

An *Ichthus* symbol as used in the early church

What we mean when talking of someone who saves (a saviour), is however likely to be very different from the ideas which the early Christians first believed.

In order to respond to some of the following questions which consider the various approaches you might find it helpful to refer to the sections on *Salvation*, and *the Cross* in the Further Reading section.

- *Do you find that what happens on the Cross helps you to think of Jesus as a saviour?*
- *Why do you think that having 'faith in Jesus' means that our sins are forgiven?*

Look at the famous hymn given below, 'There is a green hill far away', which is often sung in churches at the time when Christians recall the events of the last week in Christ's life, particularly Good Friday. Do you find this hymn helpful in its depiction of the events at Easter time?

There is a green hill far away
  Outside a city wall,
Where the dear Lord was crucified,
  Who died to save us all.

We may not know, we cannot tell
  what pains He had to bear;
but we believe it was for us
  He hung and suffered there.

He died that we might be forgiven,
  He died to make us good.
That we might go at last to heaven,
  Saved by His precious blood.

There was no other good enough
  To pay the price of sin;
He only could unlock the gate
  Of heaven and let us in.

O dearly, dearly has He loved
  And we must love Him too.
And trust in His redeeming blood
  And try His works to do.

Church Hymnary (3rd Edition) No. 241
Cecil Francis Alexander, 1818-95

Having looked in the Further Reading section at some of the ways in which Jesus is portrayed on the Cross, is there one image or a combination of images that you find particularly helpful? You might consider the Cross as a place of sacrifice, of victory, of punishment, of love, or of God's suffering.

For many of the early Christians there was an intimate relationship between what Jesus said and what he did. His words were lived out in his actions. This was especially the case in his ministry of healing.

We live in a world very different from that of Jesus and it can be difficult to come to terms with some of the events described in the New Testament. Too easily we can use the word 'miracle' to describe those occurrences for which we have no explanation. Jesus himself warned people about trusting in signs and wonders.

There were many people at the time who performed 'miracles', who claimed to be able to heal individuals. Yet the way in which Jesus healed and the purpose behind his healing was unique. This was the reason that many of the earliest Christians emphasised Jesus' ministry of healing.

There are various elements involved in the healing miracles of Jesus which help to illustrate his character. The first thing to note is that there is a very close relationship between healing and wholeness (the state to which we return after healing), and the idea of salvation. To be saved is to be returned to wholeness, and a right relationship with God. Indeed, in the Greek language of the New Testament the actual words used for healing and salvation are closely linked: to be healed is, in effect, to be made whole.

Look at some of the healing stories of Jesus

- *Share with one another your reactions to these events.*
- *What is happening in each story?*

Mark 1:40-44

Mark 5:21-34

Luke 11:14-19

John 9:1-12

Think carefully about the way in which Jesus relates to the people involved.

There are key characteristics involved in Jesus' acts of healing. Included amongst these are the fact that he is very physical in his healing: he touches the unclean and lepers, he uses spittle to make a poultice. When people are healed a restoration takes place. For some people this means a return to community and relationship - the leper returned to acceptance; the woman who is haemorrhaging is made clean and returns to her family; the blind man returns to worship in the Temple.

The healings always point to the glory of God. It is not that Jesus is unique as a healer - this kind of thing was believed to happen a lot in the view of first century inhabitants - it has more to do with the people he healed and the result of the healing, all of which point to his words and the message he communicates about the kingdom of God.

The early Church found it difficult to cope with this dimension of Jesus' ministry. The understanding of healing changed at an early stage in the Church's history and the more dramatic ministries and gifts of healing became less commonly spoken of. Healing was considered to be a gift which was possessed by only a few.

Now think about your own lives and the community in which you live.

- *Are there situations there where there is need of healing, restoration and reconciliation?*
- *Talk with one another about what these might be.*
- *Do you think there is anything in the way in which Jesus healed that might help these situations?*
- *Does the idea that Jesus heals and restores to wholeness have a particular meaning in your life?*

Jesus the servant

The emphasis in the New Testament on Jesus the servant is closely associated with Jesus the healer.

This was a significant development in the traditional view of God. Throughout the New Testament there is an emphasis in Jesus' ministry and teaching on service and lowliness, given the nature of his leadership.

Perhaps the service of Jesus as the Christ is summed-up best in the moments in the Upper Room. Jesus spends time with his disciples directly before he is betrayed and he is seen washing the feet of his disciples. In the Jewish culture of the time such an action was only undertaken by the lowest member of the household, usually a female slave. Here we find Jesus warning his disciples that unless they allow him to act in such a way they cannot belong to him and his kingdom. This was a hard thing for the early Christians to understand, especially after the events of the Resurrection, believing that this had glorified Jesus.

Look at the picture on ***page 88****.*

- *How do you respond to it?*
- *What words come into your mind to describe this?*

Share these with others.

How comfortable are you with the idea of Jesus as someone who serves you?

- *How does this fit in with some of the ways in which we talk about and to Jesus in church - in our prayers and in our hymns?*
- *Does Jesus the servant fit into the image many people have of him?*

Uniquely in St John's Gospel, the washing of the feet is the central element in the Last Supper story. The idea of having a foot-washing service instead of communion sadly would not go down well in many churches!

Jesus the Messiah

The Messiah, which is in effect the same term as Christ and means 'the anointed one', was a very powerful political word in the world of first century Israel. To a people suffering under the oppression of a foreign power, the Messiah was the awaited great king from the line of David who would bring back the Jewish kingdom.

There is controversy over whether Jesus ever referred to himself as 'Messiah', though there are indications that others did so. However Jesus did certain things, such as riding into Jerusalem on a donkey and overturning the market stalls in the temple, which fulfilled messianic prophecies of the Hebrew Scriptures.

The early Christians, such as the writer of the 4th gospel, are keen to draw a distinction between the political use of the term 'Messiah' as used in Judaism, and the Christian usage of it. The term becomes linked to the passage in Isaiah of the suffering servant:

> Surely he has borne our infirmities and carried our diseases;
> yet we accounted him stricken,
> struck down by God, and afflicted.
> But he was wounded for our transgressions,
> crushed for our iniquities;
> upon him was the punishment that made us whole,
> and by his bruises we are healed.
>
> Isaiah 53:4-5

The word 'Christian' only began to be generally used in the second century by the early followers. The term 'Messiah' was less popular amongst many in the early church because of its Jewish and very human overtones, which did not sit well with their need to emphasise the divinity of Jesus.

Jesus the Son of God

For many people the title 'the Son of God' is the main way in which they understand the relationship between Jesus and God. In reminding us of our own family ties, it helps us to understand the relationship in a very human way. This is both a strength and a weakness: it is very easy to understand, but it can also mean that we view the relationship between Jesus and God in too simplistic a way.

At the time of Christ, 'the Son of God' was a title which was just beginning to come to be linked with the term 'Messiah'. Nevertheless even the writers of the New Testament had a problem with this term. They were not sure what it meant and how the Messiah would be related to God, so many of them didn't use this expression.

It is however clear, despite problems with the expression, that Jesus considered himself to have a close relationship with God. Indeed many of those around him were offended and shocked at the intimacy with which he spoke to Yahweh. In prayers Jesus calls God 'Abba' which is a very familiar expression, more Dad than Father.

For the early church, using the phrase 'the Son of God' helped them to understand the God-like part of Jesus' nature. One of the big struggles both in the New Testament and in the early Church was the attempt to balance the two very remarkable and very different statements that Jesus is at one and the same time both God and a human being.

Jesus the Lord

The depiction of Jesus as 'Lord' is perhaps the earliest Christian confession of faith. When early Christians were baptised they took a vow which proclaimed that they believed Jesus was Lord.

The word has a special place because it has many different meanings associated with it. The Greek word from which we get the term 'Lord' is *kyrios*, and it is equivalent to the holy name of God in the Hebrew Scriptures, Yahweh. By describing Jesus as Lord the early Christians are saying very clearly who they believe him to be.

Yet despite its very common use amongst people today, what does the word 'Lord' communicate in our time? With its connotations of hereditary privilege/ aristocratic titles, it is at risk of becoming an out-moded term in our society. We live less and less in a society where people are given special status because of being born into particular families. The power, virtually of life and death, which medieval lords had is no longer a reality. The term has increasingly come to have negative associations, e.g., 'he lords it over others', 'who do you think you are, my Lord and Master?'

- *What does the word 'Lord' say to you?*
- *Do you think it is a helpful way of speaking of the Jesus you know?*

Jesus the Word

In many churches you will hear reference to 'the Word'. This comes from one of the terms which was used to describe Jesus in the early Church. The most famous use of this phrase is at the beginning of John's Gospel.

> In the beginning was the Word, and the Word was with God, and the Word was God. He was in the beginning with God. All things came into being through him. And without him not one thing came into being that has come into being...
>
> And the Word became flesh and lived among us, and we have seen his glory, the glory as of the Father's only son...
>
> John 1:1-3a, 1:14a

The precise meaning of the phrase which is translated as 'word' (the Greek word *logos*) is unclear. We would understand this term a lot better if we were first century Greek citizens. The term 'word' had significance not only in the Greek world but also in the Jewish world.

When we hear the phrase 'the Word', the first thing which might come to our mind is the Bible. Strictly speaking the Bible is not the Word of God but points to the Word of God, who is Jesus Christ. You might find it interesting to trace the way in which this term came to be used by looking at some of the Further Reading section on **page 155**.

For our purpose here it provides a good example of the way in which early Christians sought to describe Jesus Christ in words and ways which would speak to the people around about them.

Share with one another the words which might or might not be used in scripture, but which you would use to speak to someone about Jesus:

- *for example, would you describe him as a teacher, as a personal friend, a rebel, a role model, an anarchist, a madman?*

- *How important is it that we try today to speak of Jesus in different ways which communicate to people around us?*

Look at the pictures on ***page 89****: do any of them help you to answer the question:*

'Who do you say that I am?'

We live today in communities where there are many different beliefs and faiths. One of the traditional aspects which Christianity has emphasised is the uniqueness of Jesus. The way in which he is unique is something therefore which is important for us to think about.

> Jesus said to him, 'I am the way, and the truth, and the life.
> No one comes to the Father except through me.'
>
> John 14:6

- *In what way do you think Jesus might have been unique and special?*

Many people find it is through the hymns we sing, the pictures we see and the poems we read that we gain a deeper insight for our understanding of Jesus.

- *So would the real Jesus please step forward... who is he for you?*

Share your reactions to any of the thoughts in Further Reading.

The HOLY SPIRIT

What is spirit?

There are many different ways of picturing and understanding the Spirit: in this unit we shall examine some of the ways the Spirit has been understood in the Old Testament, in the New Testament and in the Church since that time.

First of all we would like you to share with one another occasions when you would use the word 'spirit', whether in a religious sense or not.

- *When people talk of the 'triumph of the human spirit', what do you think is meant by that?*
- *What words would you use to describe this spirit?*
- *Where does this spirit come from? Inside us or outside?*
- *Where do you feel it? In your heart, in your gut, in your mind?*

Can you think of an example - either from a story you have heard or someone you know of - demonstrating resilience of spirit?

Now share with one another what you think is meant by the term 'the Holy Spirit'.

- *What do you consider are the differences or similarities between the 'spirit' and the 'Holy Spirit'?*

Look at the photographs on ***page 92****.*

- *What makes you think of 'spirit', whether human or holy, in these?*
- *Now write down in words, or draw in pictures, images which you could use to try to describe the Holy Spirit.*

Ideas of the Spirit in the Old Testament

In Jewish writings, the Spirit is seen in a variety of ways.

The Spirit as *ruach*.

Ruach is an important Hebrew word which can be translated as wind, breath or spirit. In the sense of 'wind', in hot Mediterranean climates especially, wind is a powerful image - at the same time something refreshing yet powerful, and occasionally frightening. In the sense of 'breath', it contains the idea of the spirit as associated with what gives life. The breath of God is a life-giving spirit present in creation and in the creating process itself. For the writers of the Hebrew Scriptures of the Old Testament, the image of God as Creator and Maker was one which was powerfully conveyed by the idea of the *ruach* of God, drawing on these associations.

Looking at picture 1 on ***page 93****, consider how you see the Spirit of God as moving in creation:*

- *as a one-off in the creating process?*
- *as something still continuing now?*

How do you think this fits with a scientific account of the origins of the world?

Close your eyes and take a few deep breaths, breathing in through your nose and out through your mouth. Sit quietly for a few minutes and listen to your normal breathing pattern.

- *Can you feel the breath of God move through you?*
- *How did that quiet exercise make you feel?*

Look at the following poems about creation. Consider which one most appeals to you. What does it say to you about the creative Spirit?

In the beginning, God made laughter

He made it for Adam,
when the winter came
and the leaves started to wither;

He made it for Eve,
when her children asked
where their mum came from;

He made it for Methuselah,
when the time came to blow out the candles
on his birthday cake;

He made it for Mrs Noah,
when her husband first mentioned
his amphibious zoo;

He made it for Abraham,
when, a year off a hundred,
he was asked to walk the world;

He made it for Sarah,
when she eavesdropped on an angel
and giggled until she was pregnant;

He made it for Moses,
when the sheep raised their heads
in confusion at his stutter;

He made it for Miriam,
when she danced on dry land
as a sign of liberation;

He made it for wee David,
when Saul offered to make him
the youngest lance-corporal;

He made it for big Goliath,
when he first glimpsed the cause
of impending rigor mortis;

God made laughter for himself,
when his children on earth
took themselves too seriously;

And he gave it to Jesus,
to share with his friends,
to use in his stories,
to praise in young children,
to bring to the sad.

So, we dare not, in our wisdom,
doubt that God inhabits humour,
nor condemn him to be dour
like some bankrupt undertaker.
From his Spirit issues joy,
and that fruit is for our healing.

From *Flowing Streams,* ed. Donald Hilton

God's Grandeur

The world is charged with the grandeur of God.
It will flame out, like shining from shook foil;
It gathers to a greatness, like the ooze of oil
Crushed. Why do men then now not reck his rod?
Generations have trod, have trod, have trod;
And all is seared with trade; bleared, smeared with toil;
And wears man's smudge and shares man's smell: the soil
Is bare now, nor can foot feel, being shod.

And for all this, nature is never spent;
There lives the dearest freshness deep down things;
And though the last lights of the black West went
Oh, morning, at the brown brink eastward, springs -
Because the Holy Ghost over the bent
World broods with warm breast and with ah! bright wings.

Gerard Manley Hopkins 1844-89

The Spirit as a source of inspiration and power

Throughout the Old Testament, as well as being a source of creation and creativeness the Spirit is envisaged as a source of inspiration, for prophets, priests and kings. Such inspiration is frequently associated with a sense of power. This power is experienced as being granted to individuals for the purpose of bringing the community closer to God.

So we find accounts in the Old Testament which show people being inspired by God's Spirit:

- Inspiring Israel's heroes in battle (such as Samson)
- Inspiring artistic genius (Exodus 35:31, 'he has filled him with divine spirit, with skill, intelligence, and knowledge in every kind of craft')
- Inspiring understanding and insight (as in the story of Joseph)
- Inspiring the ruler and lawgiver (such as David and Solomon)
- Inspiring prophecy (Isaiah 61:1, 'The spirit of the Lord God is upon me, because the Lord has anointed me; he has sent me to bring good news to the oppressed, to bind up the broken-hearted, to proclaim liberty to the captives, and release to the prisoners')
- Inspiring wisdom (Deuteronomy 34:9, 'Joshua son of Nun was full of the spirit of wisdom, because Moses had laid his hands on him; and the Israelites obeyed him, doing as the Lord had commanded Moses').

This filling of an individual with the Spirit is known as 'charism'. Scriptural writers were very conscious that when individuals acted in a way that was of benefit to the community, this would happen because God's Spirit was at work through them and their actions. If they acted in ways which harmed or hindered the community, then those actions were considered as not being of the Spirit.

- *Consider some prominent and inspirational figures: do you have a sense that the Spirit of God is working through them?*

The Spirit as God's presence in the covenantal community.

The Spirit of God was seen not only as a source of inspiration for individuals, whether kings, prophets or artists: the Spirit also had an intimate relationship with the entire community of the people as a whole.

One of the things which marked Israel out from other peoples was their conviction that God had entered into a special relationship with them through the covenant (a promise with responsibility on both partners) described in Exodus and Deuteronomy. The presence of God with his pilgrim people was what had sustained them throughout their years travelling in the wilderness until they came to the land of promise.

Thereafter, the Hebrews believed that one of the actions of the Spirit was to show the continued presence of God amongst his people. When the people failed or turned away from God, then the images used were often those which suggested that returning to God would lead to spiritual as well as national renewal. Perhaps one of the most famous examples of this sense of the Spirit of God renewing a people is found in the story of the Valley of Dry Bones in Ezekiel:

> The hand of the Lord came upon me, and he brought me out by the spirit of the Lord and set me down in the middle of a valley; it was full of bones... He said to me, 'Mortal, can these bones live?' I answered 'O Lord God, you know'. Then he said to me, 'Prophesy to these bones, and say to them: O dry bones, hear the word of the Lord'.
>
> ...Then he said to me, 'Prophesy to the breath, prophesy, mortal, and say to the breath: 'Thus says the Lord God: Come from the four winds, O breath, and breathe upon these slain, that they may live'. I prophesied as he commanded me, and the breath came into them, and they lived, and stood on their feet, a vast multitude.
>
> Ezekiel 37:1, 3-4, 9-10

Do you think your community shows the Spirit of God in its work? If not, what 'dry bones' might need renewing for it to do so?

The Spirit as feminine

The word for spirit in Hebrew is a feminine word. She is referred to as such in the hymn which follows. The hymn also picks up on some other important biblical images of the Spirit.

She sits like a bird, brooding on the waters,
hovering on the chaos of the world's first day;
she sighs and she sings, mothering creation
waiting to give birth to all the Word will say.

She wings over earth, resting when she wishes,
lighting close at hand or soaring through the skies;
she nests in the womb, welcoming each wonder
nourishing potential hidden to our eyes.

She dances in fire, startling her spectators
waking tongues of ecstasy where dumbness reigned;
she weans and inspires all those whose hearts are open,
nor can she be captured, silenced or restrained.

For she is the Spirit, one with God in essence,
gifted by the Saviour in eternal love;
she is the key opening the scriptures,
enemy of apathy and heavenly dove.

From *Enemy of Apathy* (Wild Goose Publications, 1988)
John L Bell and Graham Maule

- *How do you feel about the female images?*
- *Do you usually think of the Spirit in terms of maleness or femaleness?*
- *Does the description of the Spirit's actions in the song fit in with your idea of the role of the Spirit?*

This hymn also combines some of the traditional images of the Spirit, from both Hebrew and Christian scriptures; such as:

mother bird

As an eagle stirs up its nest, and hovers over its young; as it spreads its wings, takes them up, and bears them aloft on its pinions, the Lord alone guided him...

Deuteronomy 32:11-12

dove

And when Jesus had been baptized, just as he came up from the water, suddenly the heavens were opened to him and he saw the Spirit of God descending like a dove and alighting on him.

Matthew 3:16

fire

Divided tongues, as of fire, appeared among them, and a tongue rested on each of them.

Acts 2:3

- *Are any of these similar to the images and pictures which you developed earlier?*

The Spirit in the New Testament

When we turn to the New Testament, there are particular developments which complement the historical Jewish understanding of the Spirit.

One of the key events of the New Testament is the baptism of Jesus: and at that baptism we find the Spirit playing a prominent role. There is a sense in the telling of the story - for instance in Matthew 3:16-4:1 - that Jesus is *empowered* by the Spirit.

Look at picture 2 on ***page 93****: water has always been an important image for the Spirit. Share with one another what ideas on the Holy Spirit come to your mind when you look at the picture.*

The empowering of the Spirit is further witnessed in the way in which the Spirit is spoken of in relation to the early Christian church. Perhaps one of the most dramatic and famous events in the Christian story is the tale of Pentecost, when the Spirit is described as coming down upon the first disciples.

> When the day of Pentecost had come, they were all together in one place. And suddenly from heaven there came a sound like the rush of a violent wind, and it filled the entire house where they were sitting. Divided tongues, as of fire, appeared among them, and a tongue rested on each of them. All of them were filled with the Holy Spirit and began to speak in other languages, as the Spirit gave them ability.
>
> Acts 2:1-4

How do you react to this story? Are you comfortable with the supernatural nature of the event?

Look at this poem:

The day of Pentecost

The path of destruction
Is all one can see
Of the riotous wind.
It rips houses
From their foundations
And plucks trees
From the ground.
It makes families homeless.
This is
Devastation.
Then there is the gentle breeze
Cooling the hot brow
In summer.
Gently rustling the green leaves.
But no wind was
So gentle
And yet
So mighty
As the coming of the Holy Spirit.

Jenny Mabbott, 14 years.

Think about the events of Pentecost.

- *Does this seem to you a disturbing or liberating event?*
- *Why do you think it is that people find it hard to accept this dramatic view of the Spirit within the institutional churches?*

However disturbing, the events of that day had a profound effect upon the first disciples; and thereafter there was an abiding sense that the presence of the Spirit represented the continuing presence of Jesus to his disciples and amongst his followers - as in 1 Corinthians 12:13, 2 Corinthians 13:13, Ephesians 4:3; and in some respects, the activity of Jesus now that Jesus was no longer there in the flesh, for instance in John 14:16, 1 John 4:1-3.

It is the Spirit also which empowers people to live a moral and ethical life. Paul stresses that the life of the Spirit is not the same as the life of the flesh - Galatians 5:13-26.

Many early Christians felt they entered into a sense of belonging to the Church through the Spirit: many 'spirit' references in the New Testament are related to its workings in baptism.

> Peter said to them, 'Repent, and be baptised every one of you in the name of Jesus Christ so that your sins may be forgiven; and you will receive the gift of the Holy Spirit'.
>
> Acts 2:38.

Fundamental to this is the recognition that this gift is only the first installment in God's complete salvation of believers.

The Spirit in relationship

After the very earliest period of Christianity, the Holy Spirit became a key element in the way in which the church sought to understand the continuing presence of Christ, and the relationship between Christ and God the Creator.

The early church had started to speak of the Spirit, of Jesus and God in its writings and in worship, and therefore wanted to make it very clear to everyone that they were not speaking of three different gods but rather of three ways to understand the one God. This was done through developing the idea of the Trinity. This idea also helped in trying to explain how God, Jesus and the Spirit related to each other and to us. The writers of the early church wanted to emphasise the belief that all three 'persons' of the Trinity were intimately linked with one another in the closest conceivable form of relationship.

Thus for many Christians, the Trinity and the relationship it describes provide the best understanding of community. By implication, this means that there is equality given to each of the members of the Trinity. It is not as if the Father is more important than the Son, the Son than the Spirit. All have equal weight - it is just that our relationship with each one is somewhat different.

The Trinity is very difficult to understand as an abstract idea, and so many of the great thinkers of the early church used pictures to help people.

Look at the clover leaf below: if you consider each leaf as standing respectively for the Father, Son and Spirit, how does this help in your understanding of the idea of the Trinity?

Alternatively, look at this picture of the sun. Try thinking of the Father as the sun itself, Jesus as the light and the heat as the Spirit: does this communicate to you an idea of the Trinity?

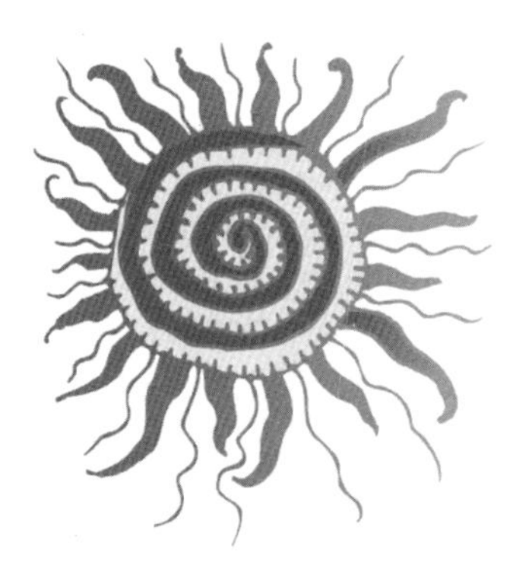

Look at these three-circle diagrams. Which of these is closest to your idea of the relationship between God, Jesus and the Spirit?

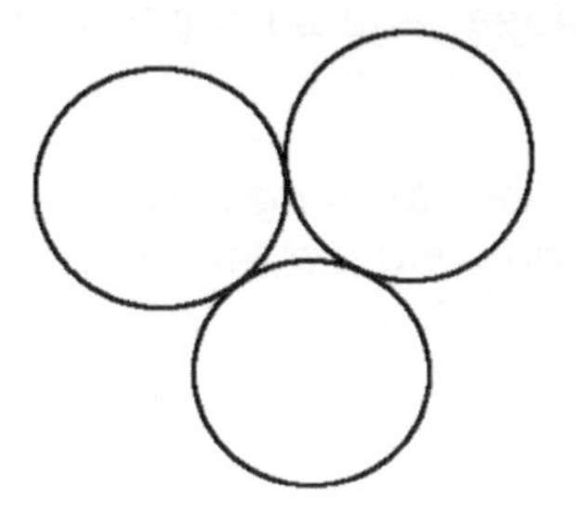

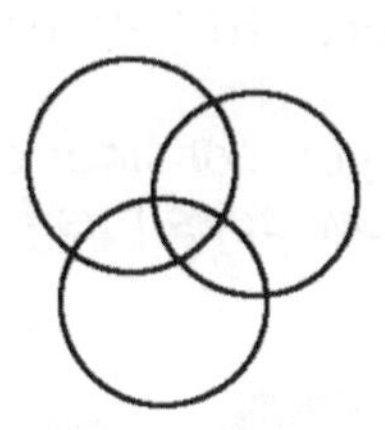

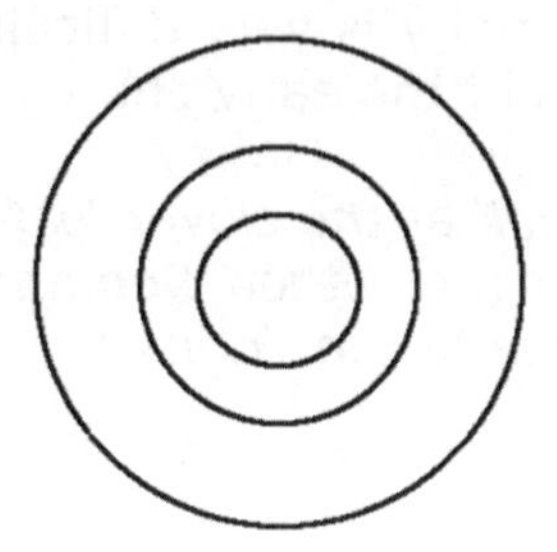

The Spirit and the Church

In the early church the work of the Spirit in the community and in individuals was frequently indicated by the presence of what came to be known as spiritual gifts. This included speaking in tongues - being moved by the power of the Spirit to speak in an unknown language, which is only understood by those who are given the gift of interpretation. It also included gifts of prophecy, and miracles. In addition there was also a general understanding that human abilities and gifts were the fruit of the Spirit's activity:

> Now there are varieties of gifts, but the same Spirit; and there are varieties of services, but the same Lord; and there are varieties of activities, but it is the same God who activates all of them in everyone. To each is given the manifestation of the Spirit for the common good. To one is given through the Spirit the utterance of wisdom, and to another the utterance of knowledge according to the same Spirit, to another faith by the same Spirit, to another gifts of healing by the one Spirit, to another the working of miracles, to another prophecy, to another the discernment of spirits, to another various kinds of tongues, to another the interpretation of tongues.
>
> 1 Corinthians 12:4-11

From about the fifth century until the early twentieth century, spiritual gifts such as miracles, prophecy, speaking in tongues, healing, and exorcism were only generally demonstrated in small non-mainstream sects, or in exceptional people, many of whom were called saints.

It was not until 1906 that members of some wider churches began to experience these gifts as a part of their regular worship. From a congregation in Los Angeles these spiritual gifts spread across America, leading to the birth of Pentecostalism, a movement which believed that it was re-discovering the gifts of the Holy Spirit.

Gradually a set of teachings arose stressing the sinful nature of the world and the need for a separate Christian identity within it; since it was believed that all aspects of culture could be 'Christianised', i.e. could become a vehicle for the Spirit - and the reverse - from businesses to television. From the 1960s onwards the charismatic revival, as it came to be called (from *charismata*, the Greek word for gifts), stressed the importance of what people experienced over and against what could be explained rationally. In the UK the revival has spread across all denominations and become less limited to one grouping than in America. In the last twenty years there have been significant shifts within the charismatic movement, generally pulling it towards a more 'conservative' approach: particularly in terms of its interpretation of Scripture, stress on traditional morality and conservative political involvement, with an emphasis on miraculous healing. An extreme version of this kind of association with the powers of the Spirit is the Toronto Blessing, which has arisen out of these tendencies. An 'inspirational' movement with many ardent believers, the Toronto Blessing has become associated in the popular imagination with 'odd' behavioural manifestations - for instance believers falling around and making animal noises as a possession of the Spirit. The apparent loss of control disturbs many people.

Discuss with the other members of the group how easy you find it to accept the claims of people to manifest the gifts of the Spirit through signs such as 'speaking in tongues', healing and being 'slain' in the Spirit.

- *Do you think that your church - locally or nationally - shows through its work the Spirit of God in the world?*
- *How do you think it could do so more effectively?*

The mainstream churches are often accused of having robbed the gifts of the Spirit of their power and radical edge. It has been suggested that they have become too closely linked with the establishment in society.

More recently however, there has been a feeling of the rediscovery of the Spirit as being alive and active in the natural world, in art, culture and politics. The language of spirit is becoming more common in society; and for many people outside the church who want to affirm their sense of a Holy 'Other' or divine presence, the Spirit is a way in which they can seek to talk about their experience of God.

Look at this passage written by a contemporary thinker:

> At the end of one age and at the start of a new millennium, with the world still on the brink of apparent catastrophe, with wars and rumours of wars, environmental disaster prophesied every year; the hungry still staring from our digital screens and the poor still sleeping 'rough' on our smooth streets, Christians struggle with what God plans and desires for themselves and for the creation.
>
> Those of us who live in the northern hemisphere have been used to assuming that power, whether economic, political or military, is very firmly within our hands and grasp. Even the way we speak of the countries of the southern hemisphere as 'developing' or 'third world' suggests that we view these nations as somehow inferior to our great civilisation and ideas.
>
> But hold on, what is the Spirit of God saying in these days?
>
> Is God not saying that the kingdom doesn't belong to the financiers and the business men but is to be shared by the poor and the dispossessed? Isn't God saying that the Spirit is blowing through our world to wreak havoc on our tidy and ordered complacency? Isn't God saying that the burning fire of the passionate Spirit is setting on fire all the defences we choose to put up which prevent us from really caring for our world and its peoples? Isn't God saying that the hungry are going to be filled at the table of the Kingdom and that the food they will be given will come from our groaning, obese tables? Isn't God saying that the hatred within our hearts for those of difference, whether of gender, sexual orientation or colour is a hatred which will

ultimately consume and destroy us?

I think God is letting the Spirit loose on the world and we had better watch out because the fire demands that we make the choice. Either turn and change and make a choice for life, for the poor, for those who count as nothing, for those we do not want to see. Or be burned by a judgement which will destroy the 'first world'; and make the world of the south a place of God's presence. Make a choice for the power of the Spirit or allow the structures of your security deaden your heart.

As for the Church - well the bush is burning and though we have tried, we have not tamed its fire or lessened its heat. I have no doubt that the Spirit will consume the structures of the fading institution and the Church will be re-born, and its face will be the face of the forgotten, and its words will be the lost words, and its mission will be to serve not itself but the world. The Spirit is out there, burning up our excuses and pushing us into a new path.

Yes, God's Spirit is on fire.

- *How do you react to these words?*
- *Are you comfortable with such an unpredictable force?*

Having looked at all the religious and biblical understandings and images of the Spirit outlined in this chapter, look through a newspaper and pick out two or three stories which demonstrate the Spirit to you. Or pick a piece of music or choose a picture which you would want to describe as 'spiritual'.

- *Why does it move you?*
- *What is it about it that makes it special for you?*

How much do you think that the Spirit of God works through you:

- *In your gifts and talents - do you think of yourself as having a 'God-given talent'?*
- *In your interaction with others*
- *In your work and/or personal life*
- *In helping you decide the best course to take?*

The
BIBLE

The purpose of this section is to give you some insight on the Bible as a historical document, and to discover a little more about the Bible; considering how to use it, and what it means to you.

> There's a story told of a Tanzanian woman who wandered around her village carrying an old black, worn Bible above her head. Everywhere she went she carried the Bible. The children of the village made fun of her, mocking her for carrying this old Bible. The older people thought she was strange because she would never put it down. 'Why,' they asked, 'are you always carrying that Bible? There are plenty of other books that you could read.'
>
> 'Yes' she replied, 'there are plenty of other books which I could read but this is the only book in the world that reads me.'

'This is the only book which reads me.'

- *How do you understand this statement?*
- *Is it true for you?*

The Bible is an extremely important book. Its stories and content have passed into popular culture, making it the stuff of literature, art, advertising and, at times, comedy. Even people who do not believe in its truth and or subscribe to its message are still influenced by it, since many of its teachings have passed into our law and culture. From swearing on the Bible in a court of law to Andrew Lloyd Webber musicals, the presence of the Bible is inescapable.

Anyone who comes into any contact at all with Scripture tends to make assumptions about what it contains and what it tries to do, sometimes without realising what those assumptions are. The Bible is a very rich and complex document. It is also, in a sense, a living entity with which we are in a relationship. As we grow and change, what we take from the Bible is different at each reading. Often when we re-read a familiar story after an interval, we discover that what is actually there is rather different to our rememberings.

- *How important is the Bible to you?*
- *Do you read it?*
- *How easy do you find it to read the Bible?*

A well-known story?

Whether or not they reckon to know the Bible well, there's at least one section of it which most people think is pretty familiar. We all know the Christmas story, don't we?...

Test yourself on these twenty questions:

1 Christmas has always been celebrated on the 25th December
True/False

2 Joseph was from
A. Bethlehem
B. Jerusalem
C. Nazareth
D. Egypt
E. Glasgow
F. Who knows?

3 How did Mary and Joseph travel to Bethlehem?
A. Camel
B. Donkey
C. Walked
D. Rickshaw
E. Joseph walked, Mary rode on a donkey
F. Who knows?

4 Mary and Joseph were married when Mary became pregnant.
True/False

5 Mary and Joseph were married when Jesus was born.
True/False

6 What did the inn keeper tell Mary and Joseph?
A. 'I have no room'
B. 'Come back after the Christmas rush and I should have some vacancies'
C. 'I have a stable you can use'
D. Both A and C
E. None of the above

7 Jesus was born in a

A. Stable
B. Manger
C. Cave
D. Barn
E. Unknown

8 Which animals does the Bible say were present at Jesus' birth?

A. Cows, sheep and goats
B. Cows, donkeys and sheep
C. Sheep and goats only
D. Lions, elephants and tigers
E. None of the above

9 Who saw the star in the east?

A. Shepherds
B. Mary and Joseph
C. Three kings
D. Both A and C
E. None of the above

10 What did the angels tell the shepherds to look for?

A. A star over Bethlehem
B. A baby that doesn't cry
C. A baby in a stable
D. Both A and C
E. None of the above

11 What did the angels sing?

A. 'Joy to the world, the Lord has come'
B. 'Alleluia'
C. 'Unto us a child is born, unto us a son is given'
D. 'Glory to God in the highest and peace on earth'
E. 'Glory to the new born King'

12 What is frankincense?

A. A precious metal
B. A precious fabric
C. A precious perfume
D. A monster story
E. None of the above

13 What is myrrh?
- A. An easily shaped metal
- B. A spice used for burying people
- C. A drink
- D. After-shave lotion
- E. None of the above

14 How many wise men came to see Jesus?
- A. Three
- B. Two
- C. Several
- D. Fourteen
- E. Unknown

15 What does 'wise men' refer to?
- A. Educated men, intellectuals
- B. They were eastern kings
- C. They were astrologers
- D. They were clever enough to follow the star
- E. They were sages

16 The wise men found Jesus in a
- A. Manger
- B. Stable
- C. House
- D. Inn
- E. Good mood

17 The wise men stopped in Jerusalem
- A. To tell Herod about Jesus
- B. To find out where Jesus was
- C. To ask about the star they saw
- D. For camel food
- E. To buy presents for Jesus

18 Who told Mary and Joseph to go to Bethlehem?
- A. The angel
- B. Mary's mother
- C. Herod
- D. Caesar Augustus
- E. Alexander the Great
- F. No-one

19 Joseph took the baby Jesus to Egypt

A. To show him the pyramids
B. To teach him the wisdom of the Pharoahs
C. Because he dreamt about it
D. To be taxed
E. Joseph didn't take Jesus to Egypt

20 Where do we find the Christmas story?

A. Matthew
B. Mark
C. Luke
D. John
E. All of the above
F. Only A and B
G. Only A and C
H. Only A, B and C

Scores

Over 15 correct	Excellent (better than the Minister)
10 - 14 correct	Good (the Study Group needs you)
5 - 9 correct	Lots of room for improvement (you need the Study Group)
0 - 4 correct	Rotten (don't believe everything you sing in Christmas Carols!)

1 False (only since the 4th Century)
2 A (Luke 2:3-4)
3 F
4 False (Matthew 1:18)
5 False (Luke 2:5)
6 E (No inn keeper mentioned)
7 E
8 E
9 E ('wise men' saw it -they were not kings)
10 E (Luke 2:12)
11 D (Luke 2:14)
12 C
13 B
14 E (Matthew 2:1)
15 C
16 C (Matthew 2:11)
17 B (Matthew 2:2)
18 D (Luke 2:1 & 4)
19 C (Matthew 2:13)
20 G

No one, not even the most respected of Biblical scholars, knows every word of the Bible. There is no right number of times a week to read the Bible nor does the ability to quote memorised chunks mean that your relationship with the book is of a better quality. As in the development of any kind of relationship, there's a process of getting to know more about the other, the background, and the hopes and dreams - all of this deepens the relationship. So part of building that relationship with Scripture is in becoming sensitive to the sweep of history and style which it contains.

We will now do this in the next section; and as we do that, we'll think about the different ways to approach this book 'which reads me'.

The Bible and me

Look at these statements. Which of these most closely describes the relationship you have with the Bible?

Share your answers in your group.

'I just pick up my Bible and I read what God wants to tell me from it.'

'I only really hear the Bible in church; most of the time I don't particularly listen - I've heard the stories so many times I'm sick of them.'

'I find it very comforting to hear the beautiful, familiar passages.'

'I used to read fairy stories when I was younger. I find it very hard not to think of a lot of the Bible as a fairy story.'

'To be honest it's mostly just the Gospel stories that I turn to for advice. The rest seems too difficult - a bit bloodthirsty.'

'The Bible is the Word of God. Everything in it is true. I hate it when people who call themselves Christians try to wriggle out of the difficult demands it makes on us.'

'I was in a really awful marriage, and as a Christian found it really hard to reconcile this with what I read in the Bible about divorce and re-marriage. I really struggled with how to read the Bible and still escape my terrible situation.'

When we read and hear the Bible, often without realising it, we decide on, or are given, different ways in which to approach it. In the section that follows we look at some of these different methods. After you have looked at a number of methods you may want to consider which approach is most commonly taken by you, individually and in your church.

Composition

First we will look briefly at how the Bible was put together - a more detailed study is contained within the Further Reading on **page 156**.

The books

The Bible is not a single book. It is a collection of books from a wide variety of ages and cultures, and in a variety of styles. The writings contain history, poetry, prophecy, song and moral tales. The Old Testament, which we also refer to as the Hebrew Scriptures, conveys the story of God's relationship with the Jewish people before the time of Jesus. This was written in Hebrew, like the sentence underneath, a language which is hard to translate - not least because it has no punctuation or vowels!

בְּרֵאשִׁית בָּרָא אֱלֹהִים אֵת הַשָּׁמַיִם וְאֵת הָאָרֶץ׃ וְהָאָרֶץ א 2
הָיְתָה תֹהוּ וָבֹהוּ וְחֹשֶׁךְ עַל־פְּנֵי תְהוֹם וְרוּחַ אֱלֹהִים מְרַחֶפֶת

It is also hard for us to fully understand the mind-set of a people who lived so long ago, and who not only had different customs and laws but who sought things so different from our expectations from their writings. For instance, when they wrote an historical account, their desire was not to produce our kind of history - seeking the most 'reliable' account, a record filled with facts and figures - but rather they wanted to tell the story of God's relationship with his people. But however difficult this process of understanding the Hebrew Scriptures might be, it is a journey which is worth undertaking as it is the collection of sacred writings which Jesus used and which underpins our Christian faith.

The writings included in the Old Testament were written over a period of a thousand years, and can be seen to comprise five sections - history, law, poetry, prophecy and wisdom.

History

Genesis means beginning. Though the Old Testament books did not have titles, the word suggests the theme of the whole book. It is about the beginning of the universe, of humanity and of God's relationship with us. Though it is a 'first' book it was not the earliest to be written. In the form we know now, it came together in the period of time after the Jewish people had returned from exile in Babylon in c. 580 B.C.E. (Before the Common Era).

One of the reasons why it was produced at this time was in reaction to the stories of the local Canaanite people, who had different tales about the way in which the earth was made and who had beliefs in many gods. Israel wanted to celebrate her conviction that there was one God, Yahweh, who had created all the known and unknown world, who had entered into a special relationship (or covenant) with Israel, and who had been with them throughout their history.

Look at the first chapter of Genesis.

- *How do you react to this familiar version of the story?*
- *Is this best described as a poetic description of what God is doing or is it a true depiction of creation?*
- *What do you think the writer thinks that he is doing here?*
- *What does the story say to you about what God is like?*
- *Does this account of God appeal to you?*

If you go on to look at Genesis 2, you will discover there a very different tale about the start of creation. The writer is using a different technique - a story - to explore the relationship between God and humanity.

The approach given above - of looking at a chapter and then asking questions based on a personal reaction - is probably one of the most commonly used when people read the Bible in groups, such as in a Bible Study. It asks you to know a little bit of the background to a passage and attempts to balance this with your opinion and the world in which you live.

Law

There are many parts of the Old Testament which contain laws and regulations relating to how to be a true follower of Yahweh. Some of these we try to follow to this day, many of them have fallen into disuse. Some are considered to be more important than others, but there is evidence of the fact that not every word of Scripture was given the same weight even by the earliest readers.

The compilers and writers of Scripture wanted to say something about God and what it meant to be a follower of God; so as that relationship changed, then so too did the ethical and moral demands placed upon the people of God.

Look at this following true story; then read Exodus 21:12-19.

Since 1977, when Gary Gilmore was shot by firing squad in Utah, marking the re-establishment of the death penalty in America after a five-year moratorium, 616 people have been executed. And the pace is accelerating.

The legal arguments over high profile Death Row prisoners are all about process and the law. None of them is founded on the moral basis for state-sponsored execution itself. Indeed, the death penalty is almost a non-issue in the US despite vocal opposition from human rights groups, the Vatican and foreign governments. Abolitionists believe the only way to win the argument is to ram home the flawed way in which the death penalty is both handed down and carried out. 'The moral question is not one you are going to change peoples' minds about' Allyson Collins says. 'You have to convince them the safeguards are not in place to prevent innocent people being sentenced to death or guilty people being sentenced to death because they were incompetently represented by counsel who should have argued for life in prison instead'.

For as long as America believes overwhelmingly in the death penalty, politicians will not go near the issue. There is little or no debate, and no political will to start one for as long as politicians regard it as political suicide to take a stand. The last one to do so was Robert Kennedy, who said before his murder in 1968: 'Whenever any American life is taken by another unnecessarily - whether it is done in the name of law or in defiance of law... in an attack of violence or in response to violence - the whole nation is degraded'.

Adapted from a recent newspaper article

- *How helpful do you find the Bible passage in helping you to decide your response to the story?*
- *Are there other influences which affect your view on the news story?*

Many people, come to the Bible because they're looking for an answer to a question. The difficulty is that we can't simply read straightforward answers from the Bible to many of today's ethical choices. The Bible often does not present one straightforward and clear answer to a problem. Different texts suggest a variety of responses, or we have to use our own interpretation to try to understand what the Bible is saying. So, although we might say on the one hand that the Bible is fundamental to our approach to life and that it is wholly truthful, we can controvert this by choosing only texts that confirm our opinions, or by ignoring the Bible all together when it doesn't 'fit'.

- *How do you think you should use Scripture in making up your mind on difficult decisions?*

Poetry

Many parts of the Old Testament are written in poetical form. The psalms are the most famous example of such writing: they are rich in imagery and metaphor. Some of the language can be difficult, and, like all poetry, conveys different levels of meaning. However the most demanding passages are often the most powerful to read, because the individuality and personal quality of their writing bridges the gap of years between us and the writer.

Look at Psalm 142.

- *Does it express any feelings you have had?*
- *Does it help you to know such words are in Scripture?*

The approach we have just taken with this psalm is perhaps the most common when reading Scripture on our own. We read, looking for inspiration and encouragement and emotional support, without necessarily wanting to grapple with intellectual issues such as when and where it was written. It is one of the strengths of Scripture, along with much great poetry, that people are able to gain such insight from texts which are centuries old.

Prophecy

We tend to think of prophecy as the ability to foretell the future - a kind of mystical power with associations of horoscopes, crystal balls and so on. However, prophecy in the Old Testament has quite a different meaning. The section of the Bible known as 'the prophets' encompasses much of Israel's history, and is written by people who were specially chosen by God, frequently priests, who were given the task by God of warning the people of their failure to be faithful to God, and of the consequences of this. The prophets give priority to justice and integrity. In the interest of returning people to a right observance of the covenant with God, they speak out against all forms of worship and practice which do not have regard for social justice. They were allowed a measure of free speech because it was believed that they spoke the words of God. Their words were considered by Israel to be particularly relevant for the time in which they spoke; but since then, passages from their writings have often also been associated with situations occurring long after the death of the prophet.

*Look at the photographs on **page 96**.*

The following are words from the prophet Isaiah which Christ used in his preaching:

> The spirit of the Lord God is upon me, because the Lord has anointed me; he has sent me to bring good news to the poor and oppressed, to bind up the broken-hearted, to proclaim liberty to the captives, and release to the prisoners.
>
> Isaiah 61:1-2; Luke 4:18-19

- *Do these words from Scripture, written so long ago, have anything to say today to people in similar situations?*

This is one way of using the Bible creatively: using contemporary images, pictures and events to challenge us and enable us to look afresh at well-known Bible passages. We are all of us familiar with images of starvation and death and suffering - perhaps we become over-familiar, to the extent that we develop 'compassion fatigue'. The prophetic tradition of Scripture is an attempt by God to call his followers back to right living, to concerns for those who are marginalised and neglected, those of no account.

It is a continuing challenge for those who read Scripture to discover for themselves in their own culture and context what the sharp and forceful words of the prophets have to say for them.

Wisdom

Wisdom is another word with a rather different meaning today. In Scripture, the term is used to describe a body of literature: this sits alongside the body of the laws which we looked at earlier, but its concerns and background are entirely different. Developed among the sages (or wise speakers) of the royal court, it is concerned with the practical business of how to live well and wisely in an 'ordinary' settled life. God certainly features in this literature, but its understanding of God is varied and often contradictory. The wisdom literature comes from different times in Israel's history. This is reflected in a style varying from very simple, pithy, almost child-like sayings reflecting practical common sense, to very beautiful and ornate phraseology - but with its messages still essentially practical and down-to-earth.

General conclusions

Most readers find that the Old Testament contains some of the most challenging writing in the Bible. Yet at the same time it contains some of the most familiar stories in popular culture. Because of this familiarity, stories can sometimes be treated at an almost child-like level - as in the stories of David and Goliath or Joseph's dreams - and therefore lose their power.

The other thing which can happen when only parts of Scripture are well known and familiar is that the more difficult passages are neglected and ignored so that we get a 'sanitised' view of God. For instance, when the pop group Boney M chose to turn Psalm 137, 'By the rivers of Babylon', into a song, they missed out the last two verses prophesying the destruction of Babylon - yet it is the whole psalm and not just part of it which is a description of God and his relations with his people. Some of the methods suggested in this unit may help in trying to tackle some of the more challenging passages in different ways.

In the centuries after the Hebrew Scriptures of the Old Testament were finalised, and before the time of Jesus, there continued to be a great many religious writings produced. For many reasons, these works didn't find their way into the Hebrew canon (a selection of books accepted as having a particular authority for the religious community). However, some of these books have been collected together and are referred to as inter-testamental books; they are also known as the Apocrypha.

The New Testament

The New Testament can be divided into the Gospels, the letters of Paul and others, Acts - a book about the history of the early church - and the book of Revelation, an account of the apocalyptic vision of John of Patmos.

The New Testament was brought together as a result of a decision taken by several meetings of the Churches in the fourth century. At the time, some of the books we see in the New Testament today were not included, and some of those which were included were accepted only narrowly. There was particular controversy over the epistle of James (which Luther would later describe as an 'epistle of straw'), since it appeared to contradict the stress in St Paul that faith cannot be worked for, but is a gift from God, and the book of

Revelation. This process shows that the early Church struggled with what it understood as being particularly of value, although there was less dispute about the four gospels.

The Gospels

Many people are most familiar with the books of the Bible known as the gospels of Matthew, Mark, Luke and John. The first three are called the synoptic gospels and each is regarded as having a different purpose, highlighting different aspects of Jesus' ministry. St John's Gospel is remarkably different both in style and emphasis from the synoptic gospels, and probably shows his use of different traditions in his writing.

To varying extents the Gospels are the end product of a long process of people wanting to capture the words and messages of Jesus. The oral tradition of the sayings and words of Jesus were passed by word of mouth from one believer to another, from one community to another. As more and more of those who had had acquaintance of Jesus at first hand died, the need to record and to communicate the 'good news' to others in writing became more urgent. The first three gospels are closely associated with one another, and there are complex theories which describe their relationship.

Look at the following passages: Matthew 12:22-30; Mark 3:20-30; Luke 11:14-23. They tell the same story but are subtly different.

- *How does the existence of the same story in different versions make you feel?*
- *Do you think that one is more accurate than the others?*
- *Do they seem to be eye-witness accounts?*

Many works have been written by scholars to help people discover more about the language and background to the Gospels and other biblical books. Sometimes people feel that unless they have access to works such as commentaries (comments on each verse of a biblical book), it's difficult to understand the passage and what it means. Yet it is clear that Scripture has a power of its own, a power to communicate something of God without the assistance of other writings to comment on or illuminate it. For this reason Christian communities around the world, especially in Latin America, have sought to read their own story into Scripture, to make it their story. So for someone in a shanty town the story of resurrection is one which offers them a living, real and political hope that the powerful will be laid low and the poor lifted up.

- *Do you feel that you can understand a text without knowing all the historical background and information available from a commentary?*

John's Gospel was written much later than the synoptic gospels. We still don't know exactly when, but it probably dates from the first half of the second century CE. It is remarkably different in style from the others, though the writer was clearly aware of the synoptics, and probably other source material. But what he chooses to do with his material is much more akin to the work of a playwright or poet than that of the writer of a historical account. The power of John comes from his wonderful use of language and the singularity of his picture of Jesus. Many people have found both the language and theology of John's Gospel both very moving and very powerful. He depicts an intimate and human figure but also a mystical and supernatural Jesus, at one and the same time.

Ask someone in the group to read aloud the story of the woman at the well, in John 4:1-30 - slowly and reflectively, giving time for you all to listen carefully. As you hear the story, try to imagine the surroundings... the smells... the heat... the noises... the colour... Try to imagine that it's you that Jesus is speaking to:

- *How do you feel at the start of the story?*
- *What changes for you as events unfold?*
- *How do you feel different at the end of the encounter?*

Talk to other people about how you felt in trying to enter into the story in this way. Was it easy? Did you feel you gained a greater insight by doing this?

The letters

There are a varied selection of letters in the New Testament but here we shall concentrate on Paul's. The letters of Paul are the oldest documents in the New Testament and were mostly written to particular churches to deal with specific situations and questions which had arisen there. Many of these were churches which Paul knew personally through his travels to them. Because of the fact that specific issues were being addressed, their tone differs: what Paul says to one church may be couched in stronger, more direct language than when he talks about a similar point to another church. The other point worth noting is that Paul's thinking changed and evolved throughout his ministry.

It is important to remember that Paul did not meet Jesus in the flesh and, like many early Christians who had not had that direct contact, he continually struggled in his writings with making the Gospel both understandable and personally meaningful for the people with whom he worked. In this, Paul's struggle is much like ours: he has heard the stories of Jesus and wants to make sense of them. But also he is much closer to the time of Christ than we are and is more familiar with the contemporary issues than we are.

Paul had a tremendous influence upon the church and the way in which it developed its practice and theology. This influence was not always positive; and not infrequently it is passages from Paul which raise questions about our response when something in the Bible is found now to be unhelpful or even detrimental.

Look at the following passage:

> To the married I give this command - not I but the Lord - that the wife should not separate from her husband (but if she does separate, let her remain unmarried or else be reconciled to her husband) and that the husband should not divorce his wife.
>
> I Corinthians 7:10-11

- *What is your response to it?*
- *Should we qualify such passages by looking at their historical context?*

Now, having looked at a range of stories and passages from the Bible such as the ones offered above in this unit, share with each other one of your favourite Bible stories or passages:

- *Why do you like it?*
- *Do you actually feel that it affects your life?*

Truth and the Bible

One of the most contentious issues, both within Christianity and in its dialogue with people of other faith traditions, is what we mean when we say that the Bible is 'the Word of God'. Our beliefs on this point determine the ways in which we feel it is appropriate to work with the Bible. It can also affect the relative importance that the Bible plays in our lives and how we balance its messages with those from society and elsewhere.

In a group discuss:

1. What does it mean to say that the Bible is 'true'?

2. Are the following all 'true' in the same way?

- *a newspaper story*
- *your favourite poem*
- *a hymn*
- *a historical account*
- *an incident which you and other people witnessed at first hand*

3. As a group, which of the following do you agree/ disagree with?

Strongly Agree (4) Agree (3) Disagree (2) Strongly disagree (1)

- God dictated the words of the Bible and these were written down exactly.
- Though human flaws in writing it down have to be taken into account, the Bible provides us with teaching and stories which tell us all we need to know about God.
- When I find a passage from the Bible speaks to me, it's because God inspires it in that second - though it might not strike others in the same way.
- God speaks through many writings now and in the past: the Bible is only a small part of this process, with nothing distinctive except its history of being revered as sacred texts.
- Other religious writings from other traditions also contain knowledge of God - for instance the Koran.

How good is your Hebrew, Aramaic or Greek?

Most of us read the Bible in some form of translation. Most of the Bible was originally passed on by word of mouth before being written down. The Old Testament was written originally in Hebrew although it has been translated into Greek as so many people of the early church would have been more familiar with that language. The New Testament is written in Greek, although Jesus would have spoken Aramaic.

It is always very difficult to translate from one language into another and the different translations used can alter meaning quite a lot. Nowadays there is quite a choice of versions, which vary in the way translation is approached and the emphasis that translators choose to make.

Look at the following verses from different translations:

Genesis 1:1-2: The Story of Creation

Good News Bible (Illustrated Bible)
In the beginning, when God created the universe, the earth was formless and desolate. The raging ocean that covered everything was engulfed in total darkness, and the power of God was moving over the water.

Good News Bible
In the beginning God created the heavens and the earth. The earth was a vast waste, darkness covered the deep, and the spirit of God hovered over the surface of the water.

The Revised English Bible
In the beginning, God created the heavens and the earth. The earth was a vast waste, darkness covered the deep, and the spirit of God hovered over the surface of the water.

The Children's Bible
Long ago,. before time began, our world was dark and desolate.

The King James Version
In the beginning God created the heavens and the earth. And the earth was without form, and void; and darkness was upon the face of the deep. And the spirit of God moved upon the surface of the waters.

- *Which is your favourite of these versions?*
- *How much do you feel the meaning is changed by the different translations?*
- *Do you think it is valid to translate the Bible into modern inclusive language - even if this means that we move further away from the original text?*

The Bible lives

Right at the start we told the story of the Tanzanian woman who felt that the Bible was the only book which was able to read her. We talked of having a relationship with the Bible, something which allows movement and change to take place.

We stand nearly two to three thousand years away from most of the writings in our Scriptures. Some people believe that many things which have been written since speak to us at least as powerfully about God's continuing relationship with the people of the world. In our own lives we have stories of encounters with God and Christ, often without the space or opportunity to share with others in worship or in the life of the faith community.

- *Do you feel that the special reverence with which we regard the Bible can be unhelpful in trying to communicate God's continuing relationship with the world?*
- *How can we create spaces within our churches to listen sensitively to the new stories all around us?*

Are there other writings - stories, poetry, drama, philosophy, scientific texts - which speak to you as powerfully as the Scriptures, which you feel tell you about God as the Bible does?

PRAYER

In this section we will examine prayer: its nature, its function, its place in our lives and the Christian understanding of prayer.

This section will give you space to explore some of the questions which people have about prayer. It will do so by looking at the way in which different people have understood prayer and what happens when we pray; considering prayer both in and outside church and sharing different types and ways of prayer.

What is prayer?

Prayer is an important part of human experience. Everyone seems to pray on some level, particularly in times of crisis, even though they may not profess a religious belief. There is a sense in which prayer at its most basic level is the way in which we communicate with and relate to God.

Prayer also plays a central role in Christian worship. From this, an assumption many people often make is that prayer is part and parcel of belonging to the church, and that church-going people will have a private prayer-life in addition to their public experiences of prayer. But this assumption is not necessarily true; many people, church-going or not, struggle with their ideas of what prayer is, and how to pray.

Share with your neighbour:

Do you pray?
If so;

- *How?*
- *When?*
- *Where?*
- *How often?*
- *Do you have any particular image or images you focus on in prayer?*

After sharing your answers to the questions, it may be that you have discovered that as a group you think of prayer in many different ways. For many people, both inside and outside the church, prayer raises more questions than answers. Few people have a smooth and untroubled prayer-life, where they commune with God regularly and happily, and are satisfied that they understand what 'this prayer business' is all about.

The following questions express some of the feelings which people have about prayer.

'I feel guilty that I don't pray enough. I'm sure everyone else in church prays every day. Should I feel bad about praying less?'

'Is it right to pray about my own problems when there is so much which is bad happening in the world?'

'I prayed about a problem, but nothing's changed. Was it because I didn't pray hard enough?'

'Why do I find it harder to pray on my own than with other people? When the minister prays he seems to use all the right words. How can I pray if I don't know how to talk to God?'

'Sometimes in church when the minister is saying a prayer for us all, I feel very isolated. I can't relate to his prayer - so how can it be my prayer? I need to say sorry to God before I can talk to him. Is this right?'

'What happens when my prayers don't get answered?'

Look at the following statements:

Prayer is not something that we do when we have time; it's what makes time meaningful.

Prayer is like watching football: it can be hugely rewarding, or it can leave you feeling absolutely desolate and dejected.

Prayer is a bit like going on a long holiday to somewhere you have only ever seen pictures of in magazines. It's a journey to a place where you always wanted to go, but could never get to on your own. It gives you a different perspective on reality. It shows you the world you thought you knew all about, in a new and dramatic light. Now you're in the picture.

Prayer is walking, sitting, ironing, sleeping, eating, thinking, and so on: the most profound moments when you meet God clearly may not come when you're on your knees in church or reading your Bible - they come in times spent with others, through happy times, times of great pain and loss, through times of stillness and watching. When this has happened you realise that all life is an experience of God.

Prayer is a conversation during which I learn how to be silent.

Prayer: a solemn request for help or expression of thanks addressed to God. An earnest hope or wish.
Oxford Concise Dictionary

Share with one another your reactions to these views.

- *Do any of them come close to expressing what you feel prayer is all about?*
- *Write your definition of prayer and share it with the group.*

Scripture and prayer

The Old Testament is full of prayers, showing the way in which prayer was a natural and spontaneous way for the people of Israel to relate to God. The prayers that we find there show the whole range of human emotion and experience. It is clear that the Jewish people had an expectation that God would respond and listen to their prayers. Often, the 'prayers' which we find there are not like our understanding of silent petitions to God, but are incidents when women and men struggle in conversation and in spirit with what God is asking and demanding of them. In this sense they are prayers: whether this was Abraham arguing with God over the fate of Sodom (Genesis 18:22-33), or Jacob wrestling with God (Genesis 32:24-30).

However, we find the most personal approach to God in the book of Psalms. This book contains some prayers used in the formal worship of God in the temple, alongside some very personal and individual prayers. We find the writers pouring their concerns out to God, giving thanks and rejoicing, and also expressing doubt and sorrow. The psalms were the prayer book of Jesus. The emotions we see in the psalms encompass the range of human experience: exuberance, delight, questioning, curiosity, impatience, agony, loneliness, and deep despair. In your own prayers to God, the chances are that you will want to share the same emotions and experiences.

Look at the following list. These statements contain some of the ideas from the psalms, put into modern language. They show the range of feeling of the psalmists.

- *Have you felt any of these emotions and if so have you expressed them in prayer?*
- *Would you hesitate to be as open in your prayer to God?*

1. I have shouted for help, but nothing happens.
2. How much longer must I endure trouble? How long will I be filled with sadness?
3. I have everything I need.
4. Have I kept myself decent for nothing?
5. I feel happy because you helped me.
6. My eyes have lost their brightness.
7. I feel crushed, my friends and family keep away from me.
8. The more I think, the more I worry.
9. I am so happy I could wake up the sun.
10. I was stupid and bitter and offended, and I did not understand.
11. You were good to me and then you rejected me.
12. My heart is breaking, I cannot eat.
13. I am overcome by horror. I wish I had wings and could escape.
14. I feel happy because you are full of love and forgave me.
15. Every night my pillow is damp with tears.
16. I shouted for help and you saved me.
17. Though I face death, I have no fear, because you are with me.
18. Stop hurting me, you're wounding me terribly.
19. I long for you with a thirst only you can quench.
20. Whenever I am afraid I will trust you.

Jesus and his disciples shared the long Jewish tradition of both personal and formal prayer. What marked Jesus out as different was the intimate language he used in prayer. One of the New Testament writers assumes that the followers of Jesus will pray at all times, 'without ceasing' (1 Thessalonians 5:15); the implication being that, like their Lord, his followers will live in an intimate and close relationship with God. The New Testament teaches that prayer should be offered through the name of Jesus, and is an important part of belonging to the Christian community.

Jesus taught that prayer should be discreetly offered, not given in a showy or loud way, but should be directed not just to the needs of the individual but to the concerns of the world. Jesus himself prayed on numerous occasions, considering it to be very important in his relationship with God. Perhaps the most moving example of this can be found in Jesus pleading with God in the garden of Gethsemane (Matthew 26:36-39).

The most famous prayer in the Bible is the Lord's Prayer. Now a regular feature of worship, this prayer throughout history has been seen often as a personal and individual petition rather than a prayer of the community, demanding a response from the whole church and society.

One of the difficulties in using a particular prayer a lot, however, is that the meaning and strength of the words can be lost through familiarity. This is why many Christians have tried to put Jesus' own words into contemporary language that speaks to their own situation.

Look at the version of the Lord's Prayer below:

Our Deliverer,
You are here on earth.
Your name is holy
In the hungry
Who share their food and their dreams.
Your Kingdom come,
Which will be a fertile land
Which flows with milk and honey.
Let us be obedient to your desire,
Being courageous in protest,
Even when we hurt.
You are giving us your daily bread
In the faces of others and the sounds of our people.
Forgive us
For keeping silent in the face of evil,
And for losing our vision,
For not sharing bread and wine,
Peace and power,
Among us, now.
Don't let us fall into the temptation
Of turning away from others.
Of feeling that nothing can be done.
Or striking back when we are low.
Of accepting things as they have been
Of failing to clothe the naked and feed the hungry.
But deliver us from evil.
Give us the strength to risk love
And rejection,
To take the dangerous road
Even if it is lonely and frightening,
Because we know that in our walking
You are with us
And the Kingdom is here
Which is for ever and ever.
Amen

Write out a version of the Lord's Prayer in language that is meaningful to you.

What happens when we pray?

Which of the following best describes what happens when you pray?

'God listens while I talk.'
'God and I have a conversation.'
'God talks to me.'
'I am filled with a realisation of God's presence.'
'Nothing happens at all.'
'We are both silent.'

What we think might be happening when we pray is affected by how we are feeling and what we are experiencing when we pray. But our answers might also be influenced by the picture or image which we have of the God who listens, and to whom we look to answer our prayers. Therefore the kind of relationship we feel we have with God plays a large part in our expectations of what happens when we pray.

Prayer and worship

Many people gain their feeling of what prayer should be from religious services. The prayers which we experience in worship do indeed try to reflect some of the main ways in which we relate to God and the kind of things we might wish to say to God, both collectively and in our personal prayers.

However, the way in which you understand God's response to prayer will affect what you think is happening through the various kinds of prayers that occur in worship. The following headings are the main categories of prayer which we share in worship:
Adoration - being aware of the presence of God and giving praise
Confession - declaring where we have fallen short in our relationship with God
Supplication - being sorry and asking forgiveness
Assurance of forgiveness - being made certain of God's love
Intercession and petition - through prayer seeking help for ourselves and others
Thanksgiving - giving thanks to God for all that is good in our lives and in the world.

Adoration

Adoration strictly means to rest in the presence of God. It is the opening prayer of our worship and perhaps should be where we start in our personal prayer-life. However we sometimes find this area of prayer very difficult. It can result in far too florid language, and the difficulty that people have in expressing their thoughts to someone who is so different from them. All too often there is a temptation to use superlatives for God which, rather than adoring God for what he has done in our life and the life of the world, can serve to distance us from God. It's not uncommon to feel that there has to be a wordy start to our prayer, which overtly speaks of God's magnificence - what might be referred to as the "God, you are so big" kind of prayer, which accentuates the otherness and might of God and our subsequent lowliness.

Adoration however is a much bigger idea than this. All of us have offered spontaneous prayers of adoration at some time; when the sight of a sunset takes our breath away, when we are surrounded by people we love, when we stand in a favourite place. The gasp of appreciation we give, the feeling of profound awe which affects us, is a prayer of adoration without words. It is a reminder of our place in the scale of things which does not leave us feeling low, but rather lifts us up even as we recognise that we are much smaller than the stars at which we stare in wonder.

- *If you are profoundly moved by something do you think that this is prayer?*

Confession

A regular part of many peoples' prayer-life is when they speak to God about what they feel they have done wrong or have failed to do. It is part of human nature to believe that if you say sorry for what you have done wrong - your 'sins', to use the Christian term - then you not only feel better but that the act of saying sorry is the first step towards healing a broken situation or relationship.

There are many different ways in which Christians express these feelings to God, from public acts of confession to the intimacy of confessing sins to a priest. What unites all prayers of confession is the desire to feel free and unburdened of the bad feelings and guilt that we may have. A prayer of confession is followed by the assurance that God accepts and loves us no matter what we have done. This comes out of God's love for us, but it also demands from us a new way of living and relating.

As with all elements of prayer, things have to be held in balance. There has been a historical tendency in the Church to concentrate on the unworthiness of human beings and to make people feel somewhat downtrodden as a result. Confession is about restoring us to our right relationship with God: if you fall out with the person you love, then saying sorry, although hard, helps to move the relationship on to a deeper level.

There is also a sense in which confession is not just an individual experience. As a church and as a community, we need to be aware of the ways in which we have together failed in our relationships with God and one another.

Intercession

This is probably the area of prayer which most people really mean when they talk about 'prayer'. Intercession means standing between: it is the prayer which asks God for help, asking him to intervene in our lives, recognising that God is already involved in how we live. It is also the area which causes people most difficulty, because it asks big questions about our image of God, and whether or not it is possible for God to answer our prayers at all.

> *Look at these eight images of God. These represent some of the roles God can seem to take in order to respond to our prayers.*
>
> - *Can you relate to these?*
> - *Do you think that your idea of how God listens to prayer has changed since you were a child?*
> - *Do you think that God listens to different prayers in different ways?*

So what are we doing when we make intercession? Here are some possible responses to that question:

1. We tap into the power of God to change a situation in which we want help.

This is the belief that if we pray, God will do what we wish. The instruction to pray to God for our needs is central to the New Testament.

> Ask and it will be given to you; search and you will find; knock and the door will be opened for you. For everyone who asks receives, and everyone who searches finds, and for everyone who knocks the door will be opened.
>
> Matthew 7:7-8

But this leaves us with the tension evident in the New Testament between asking for what we need and asking for help to fulfil what God requires of us. God wants us to be concerned about our relationship with him, rather than to be so concerned about physical possessions and security. This is also a constant theme both in the Old and New Testaments:

Look at Amos 5:21-24, then Luke 18:1-8

- *What do these passages tell us about how and why we should pray?*
- *What do they tell us about the God who listens and reacts?*

This tension suggests that one answer to a commonly asked question, 'Why has God not answered my prayer?' is perhaps that we are asking God for the wrong thing.

2. We pray in order to see that God is already answering our prayers.

When we pray for those suffering from famine, for instance, the answer to our prayers comes as we recognise what God demands us to do in order to meet the needs of the problem. This is therefore about awakening our senses to the answers that are around us. This approach is helpful in reminding us that an important part of intercessionary prayer is listening rather than just talking at God all the time.

A rabbi speaking on the radio told the following story: there was once a Jewish businessman who was beginning to get into financial difficulty so he went to the synagogue and prayed to God: 'Yahweh, the only way I'll survive is if I win the lottery this week. Please help me win!' The draw came - he didn't win. The next week, staring bankruptcy in the face, he again went to the synagogue and, really pleading with God, prayed, 'Please let me win the lottery and I'll donate thousands of pounds to the synagogue fund.' But again he didn't win the lottery. By the third week he was bankrupt; so he returned angrily and harangued God - who suddenly appeared and asked him why he was so angry. The businessman replied, 'I prayed and I prayed to you to help me win the lottery, but you refused to listen.' And God said, 'I did listen, and I was ready to answer your prayer - but why for goodness sake didn't you meet me half-way, and buy a lottery ticket?'

- *Do you find it easy to listen to God when you are asking for something in prayer?*

3. Intercessionary prayer is a conversation with God.

Like all conversations, both sides are involved in the talking and listening. This idea sees God not as the one who knows and decides the future, but as one who has entered into a partnership with us, so that together we can decide what is to be done. Intercessionary prayer is the planning meeting.

Therefore God may be influenced by what we say in prayer and we in turn will be changed by what we hear in prayer from God. A classic example of the way in which prayer can be like a struggle with God and a way of coming to new insights about our situation is seen in the story of Jacob and the angel in Genesis 32:23-30.

- *Are there times when you struggle with God in your prayer life?*

4. Intercessionary prayer is about developing our relationship with God.

It may be true, as Jesus told us, that God knows our needs before we ask, but God still likes to be asked. The parallel is with human relationship. We may know that someone is going to do a certain thing for us, but still if we don't ask, they can feel taken for granted and our relationship with them will suffer. Equally, if we take people for granted then we are not being true to what we feel for them in our relationship.

5. Intercession is not just an individual undertaking.

Intercession involves us in praying with other people in community, so that together we might be able to make the difference we are praying for.

Yet prayer in worship sometimes gives us mixed messages about what prayer should be like - it can seem to imply that it should be formal, done only in an attitude of reverent silence in a special place, or perhaps that it counts for more if delivered by a minister, or that it should always start and finish in a certain way and it should use words. But for intercession - and all other forms of prayer - to be valuable, it has to relate to the needs of the people whose prayer it tries to be. Intercessionary prayer is not about fleeing from the everyday world into a private world of prayer, but of using our prayers to change and affect that world.

- *Do you feel part of the communal intercessionary prayer in your congregation?*
- *Are the prayers which are said ones you can relate to?*

It is important to remember that prayer is not magic. God is under no obligation to grant what we want or ask. If we imagine that God is at the end of a telephone line, waiting to answer our every wish, then we diminish God.

In Jesus, God is shown as intimately involved in our world; and part of the good news of Jesus' coming is that he is present in our living, in all that is negative and all that goes wrong in our lives. That means that the God to whom we pray is a God who does not always have the answers but is there with us asking the questions. When we ask for something in prayer, there is a sense in which we can only ask for something which is likely to be what Christ would want for us. We cannot pray a 'prayer' which Jesus would not have prayed, since we cannot ask for something which would harm us or not help us in the long term, and sometimes it is not always possible to recognise what is to our ultimate benefit.

There's a story that during one of the dark days in Auschwitz, when a group of prisoners was being taken to be gassed, one of the prisoners turned to a rabbi and bitterly asked,

'Where is your God now? Where are all your words and prayers and your worship now?' And, as he was led along with the rest to his death, looking around at the children playing innocently in the mud, the women crying for their husbands who had become just memories in their darkness, the old rabbi turned and replied, 'My prayers are still worthwhile, because I see through them that my God is not absent but is here, walking with us into these ovens... and he will be with us when I pray at my last, hearing and healing'.

Such a story, and there are many similar ones told by people who have suffered, illustrates not only a depth of faith but also the way in which prayer and the acts of formal religion are intimately bound up with the whole of our life. The God who is present in suffering is the God who answers and listens to prayer; and conversely the God who listens to prayer will be the God who holds us through the harsh and hard times.

- *When you pray to God to ask for something, do you feel that you always get the answer you want?*
- *How does that make you feel?*

Thanksgiving

In this kind of prayer, we give thanks to God for all that he has done in our lives, our community and world.

This can be the easiest form of prayer for many people because it is relatively simple to concentrate on an awareness of what we should be thankful and grateful for in our lives. This kind of prayer also provides the opportunity in a worship service for the congregation to hear again the story of how God related to the people of Israel, and also the good news of Christ's coming - and to give thanks for this awareness.

All too often we can fall into the routine of listing the things we want to thank God for in a way which can feel like itemising a shopping list. But it is one of the insights of the psalmists that giving thanks to God should also be done when we are not feeling in a very thankful mood or when we have nothing to be thankful for. Even they, at times - as you can see from the paraphrases we looked at on **page 63** - like us, find the process of being thankful when in trouble or distress very hard. It is the gasp, the power which takes our breath away, of recognising God in all of life and thanking God for that presence.

There are many different ways in which we can pray both personally and publicly. Different people have a different understanding of what happens when we pray. So it is inevitable that people have an equally diverse number of ways in which they deepen and develop their own ways of praying to God.

Some theologians have suggested that there is a sense in which everything in life is prayer, that prayer is like breathing, that all activity is to be engaged in praying.

Look at this reading.

> ...But wait. My eyes are almost burned by what I see. There's a bowl in front of me that wasn't there before. A brown button bowl and in it some apricots, some small oranges, some nuts, cherries, a banana. The fruits, the colours, mesmerise me in a quiet rapture that spins through my head. I am entranced by colour. I lift an orange into the flat filthy palm of my hand and feel and smell and lick it. The colour orange, the colour, the colour, my God the colour orange. Before me is a feast of colour. I feel myself begin to dance, slowly, I am intoxicated by colour. I feel the colour in a quiet somnambulant rage. Such wonder, such absolute wonder in such an insignificant fruit.
>
> I cannot, I will not eat this fruit. I sit in quiet joy, so complete, beyond the meaning of joy. My soul finds its own completeness in that bowl of colour. The forms of each fruit. The shape and curl and bend all so rich, so perfect. I want to bow before it, loving that blazing, roaring, orange colour... Everything meeting in a moment of colour and of form, my rapture no longer an abstract euphoria. It is there in that tiny bowl, the world recreated in that broken bowl. I feel the smell of each fruit leaping into me and lifting me and carrying me away. I am drunk with something that I understand but cannot explain. I am filled with a sense of love. I am filled and satiated by it. What I have waited and longed for has without my knowing come to me, and taken all of me.
>
> Brian Keenan, *An Evil Cradling*

Can what is happening here be described as a moment of prayer? You might want to try out some of the different ways of praying in the section that follows.

Ideas for different kinds of prayer:

⌘ Try repeating a single word or phrase over and over, for example: 'Lord Jesus Christ have mercy on me'. Try to fit the phrase in with your pattern of breathing so that you feel that you are breathing out the prayer from a deep part of yourself. Or try to pray like this when you walk, making each step linked to the saying of a phrase. If after a time of deep stillness or concentration the phrase fades away, then let that happen. Follow your own instinct as to what feels natural and God-given.

⌘ Sit very still and begin to be aware of the feelings of each part of your body. Consciously relax and offer every part to God, in order to channel though the body God's life-giving and peace-giving power.

⌘ Read a passage from the Gospels, and try to imagine the scene as if it were happening at that very moment, with you as a part of it.

⌘ Choose a passage and read it over several times. What phrase speaks to you the most? Listen to it, repeat it, and offer it to God.

⌘ Try reading a hymn or poem you know as if it were a prayer.

⌘ Play recorded music in the background when you are engaging in silent prayer.

⌘ Pray while focusing on an object which is meaningful to you.

⌘ Look at ways to pray with others - form a prayer chain.

⌘ Think about different opportunities to pray - at meals, to mark special events, birthdays, housewarmings and so on.

⌘ Use a photo album as a stimulus for prayer, by looking at images that are important to you and focusing on the people or situations that they conjure up.

⌘ Pour your heart out to God as you would a friend, forgetting techniques.

On some suitable later occasion (perhaps the next time you meet), share your reactions in the group.

- *Did one or more of these 'work' for you?*
- *If so, was this model more meaningful for you than a more traditional approach to prayer?*

CHURCH and MINISTRY

In this section, we will seek to understand a bit more about the church, both its practical structures and systems, and also to reflect on what the church means to us, the world and to God. To help us to do this we shall examine our own ideas and preconceptions about church; some of the images of church in the New Testament; and the historical view which people have had of what the church should be like.

> Where the church is there is the Spirit of God, and where the Spirit of God is, there is the church and every form of grace, for the Spirit is truth.
>
> Irenaeus, *Against Heresies*

> There are many sheep without, many wolves within.
>
> Augustine, *The City of God*

> The church is the only institution which exists for those outside it.
>
> attrib. William Temple, former Archbishop of Canterbury

Whenever you hear the word 'church' what image comes into your mind?

- *Either: Draw a picture of what the word' church' means to you*
- *Or: share your thoughts with someone in the group.*

Many of you may have associated the church with a building, a group of people, a denomination or an institution. For many of us 'church' is what we have experienced within churches, with both positive and negative aspects.

One of the words closely associated with descriptions of the early church in Scripture is a Greek word *kuriakon*, which means 'belonging to the Lord'. In this sense, the church is those people who belong to God. Yet one thing many people struggle with at this time is how to belong to something or someone. We all of us 'belong' in very different ways; but how we belong affects the way we form relationships with those around us.

How do you feel you belong to the church?
Are there occasions when you have felt that you didn't belong to the church?
What makes someone feel that they belong to the church? Is it about:

- *being a member*
- *going along regularly*
- *identifying yourself as a Christian*

Is it about what you do outside the church building, or what you do inside the building?

Look at the following story:

> David and Margaret are on their third church. They left their first because they felt that too many of its members weren't real Christians. There seemed to be so little commitment and very little spirituality; it seemed at times little more than a social club with religious trappings. The second church seemed different. There was lots going on with a feeling of a live spirituality, and everyone seemed very friendly. After a year or so, David and Margaret got drawn into the leadership. Once there, they were horrified by what they found.There were bitter rivalries among the leaders and episodes of backbiting. The church seemed like a fruit that was good on the outside but rotten at the core. So they moved on. Their third church seemed fine, but six months ago a new minister came, and they are not happy with the ideas that she is preaching. Others in the church don't seem to mind, but David and Margaret are not at all sure they can tolerate it. They are thinking of moving on again.

Share your response to this story in the group.

- *What do the couple seem to feel their relationship to the church should be?*
- *Do you think their responses are valid?*

The New Testament

The Greek word which describes church in the New Testament is *ecclesia* - from which we get all sorts of related words such as 'ecclesiastical'. Used literally, it means a group of people 'called out' from amongst others to gather together, originally for purposes of political action. The New Testament uses the word to describe the group of Jesus' followers 'called out' together (cf. Acts 2 and 4). The word is also related to the translation of the word 'synagogue' in the Old Testament, which in its original meaning simply means a gathering of people for a particular purpose.

Often when Paul speaks of individual local communities of believers he uses the word *ecclesia* (Romans 16:1, 1 Thessalonians 1:1). He also uses the word to describe churches in a wider geographical area. But when we come to an epistle like the one addressed to the Ephesians, we see the first use of the word 'church' in a wider, more universal sense, meaning all believers everywhere in a linked unity. There we find one of the classic images for the church, the body of Christ (see Ephesians 3:6).

The body of Christ

This image is still very popular today. We probably like it because it is an image which still has relevance in modern times. Many other teaching ideas from the New Testament are based on visual images no longer part of daily life for many of us - there are not many temples or vineyards in modern Britain, but we all have and understand the image of a body. Or we like it perhaps because it clearly contains central themes which regularly reappear in New Testament pictures of the church.

What aspects and characteristics of the human body are helpful when looking at the church? Think about this and share your ideas with the group.

Loving-community

Many of the earliest Christian congregations kept in touch with each other by letter. In the letters of the New Testament, emphasis is laid upon the intimate contact of Christian with Christian in their communal encounter with the world. Philemon is a good example of this. These letters evince a great personal warmth, one which transcended and overcame the human barriers of race (Jew and non-Jew), of class and status, of previous arguments and differences of opinion.

The word used in the Greek New Testament to describe this Christian togetherness is *koinonia*; signifying (loosely) 'body-life'. It comes to stand for the warm fellowship of Christian with Christian, within their own group or congregation, and between Christian groups in their different localities.

The Christian church began with a group of thirteen people. In its early life, it flourished as a network of groups often meeting in homes or places where people worked, and later in hidden places when persecution was rife.

This sense of *koinonia* is described in the Acts of the Apostles. We find this loving community described in Acts 2, where we read of the way in which Christians shared everything they had in common with one another. They met to worship, to eat and drink together, and they shared their property. It is not for nothing that this way of being the church was later described as 'love-communism'.

As the movement grew in numbers and spread throughout the known world, the intimate contact of Christians with Christians became more complicated. New approaches to structure, authority, discipline and doctrine had to be found; and while the believers succeeded in holding together a disparate church, something of the original sense of *koinonia* was lost.

Discuss in pairs:

- *Do you think that we have lost the idea of the church as a loving community based on real relationship?*
- *How can we hold on to such an idea whilst working with the elaborate structures of organised churches?*
- *If the local church were to resurrect such a revolutionary and integral model of shared relationship, as shown by the early church, what do you think the implications would be?*

People of God

Another image frequently used for the church is that of being the 'people of God'. This image has its roots within the Old Testament where the people of Israel were frequently described as 'the chosen people of God'. One of the problems with such an image is that it can look exclusive; a temptation which Israel frequently fell into, as they remembered the privileges and forgot the responsibilities of the 'people of God'. In the New Testament we read of Christians being described as: 'a chosen people, a royal priesthood, a holy nation, a people belonging to God' (1 Peter 2:9).

Today Christian congregations can tend to act and behave as if they were separate units. Yet the New Testament makes it clear that all Christians have a responsibility to and for one another, regardless of their geographical location, social class or race (see Matthew 25:31ff, Galatians 3:28).

- *In your experience, does your local congregation demonstrate that it sees itself as part of a wider church and community?*
- *How do we avoid the temptation the people of Israel stumbled over: only looking after ourselves so that we form exclusive cliques and clubs?*

'One, holy, catholic...'

A particularly significant description for the church is found in the creeds with the words: 'one, 'holy' and 'catholic'. Let's look a litte more closely at these terms.

'One'...

The church is regarded theologically as being 'one'. This seems on first sight to be something of a dream given the real experience of many people to the contrary: the history of the visible, institutional church has been one of schism, dissension and split. Whether it be through large historical events such as the 16th century reformation, or splits affecting smaller denominations or local communities, a process of fragmentation and disintegration seems to be part and parcel of Christian belonging. Yet the creeds still celebrate the church as being one. This is a call to continue the struggle towards closer co-operation and unity between the structures and peoples of all churches. The growth of ecumenism in the 20th century and the increase in co-operation at local and structural levels point to an increased awareness that the church can only be effective in mission and in care when seeking to work together.

Almost all churches recognise baptism performed by other denominations. This is a recognition that in Christ we are all one, even though we are at present divided. Yet still some of the major denominations do not allow each other completely open access to their celebration of the Lord's Table.

There is not enough space or time in a study of this length to describe fully the institutional differences between each of the churches. But as a broad outline, suffice it to say that many of these have to do with the way each denomination orders its pattern of authority.

The four general models are:

- *Roman Catholicism:* where the government of the church is structured through bishops with a strong link to the bishop of Rome, the 'father' of all bishops, the Pope.
- *Episcopalianism:* where the key element is the diocese (a local geographical area), presided over by its bishop, including: Anglicans, Orthodox, most Lutherans, some Methodists.
- *Presbyterianism:* where authority is based on a series of 'courts', each subject to the authority of a higher court. The main regional 'court' is a meeting of elders and ministers with others which is called a 'presbytery'. This in turn sends representatives to an annual General Assembly of the church. Examples include: Presbyterians, the United Reformed Church, other Reformed churches.

- *Congregationalism:* where each congregation is autonomous in almost every way; some congregational churches have national federations, unions or meetings where decisions are taken collectively, including: Congregationalists, Baptists, and Independent Evangelical churches.

  - *Have you ever been to the service of another denomination?*
  - *How did it feel?*
  - *Do you think society in general understands the differences between the church denominations?*
  - *Which do you think is more important - working towards one church, or towards a greater celebration of variety?*

'Holy'...

Like so many sacred words, the term 'holy' has changed its meaning over a long history of use. Nowadays we tend to think of something described as 'holy' as being different, other-worldly, set-apart. While many of these connotations are appropriate, to describe the church as 'holy' should be more understood as meaning that the church is a body of people whose purpose is to worship and glorify God.

But, however holy, the church is not without its faults and failings. In the past, institutional churches have been slow in accepting responsibility for their roles in the persecution and death of thousands of people. Indeed, at the time of the Crusades millions were killed when the church became involved in 'holy wars' against Moslems; during the times of the Inquisition thousands were slaughtered during the church's attempt to make sure everyone believed the 'right things'; in witch-hunting times also many were killed when the orthodox churches persecuted minority groups and the psychologically ill, many of whom were accused of being witches. The allegation that many wars have religion behind them is not unfounded.

To describe the church as 'holy' is still to accept and repent for the shortcomings of those who are her members. The church consists of a community of people who struggle to be true and faithful to the God in whom they believe. The church is holy because it recognises its brokenness and seeks to be made whole.

The New Testament never imagines that the church is perfect. Not that it is satisfied with its imperfections: it takes vigorous action to cope with them. But the imperfections do not stop the church being spoken of in the highest possible terms by some people, even those who have little to do with it, for its care and concern in social action. And yet others tend to write off the church because it doesn't live up to the ideal. Modern Christians, too, have sometimes been a bit ambivalent about the church.

Look at the following statements:

'You might be a church-member, but unless you have the right relationship with Christ, you are not in the real church. You can be in the real church without being a member of a church at all.'

'The church is a human institution, and we have made plenty of mistakes. Sometimes it is hard to see God working in the church at all.'

'When people talk about the church they just see what is under their noses. But while that might be imperfect, the real church is invisible and it is glorious and perfect.'

'When the organised churches do things which betray God's Word, then they cease to be the real church.'

Share with one another your response to these.

In Paul's writings, to be 'in the church' and to be 'in Christ' means the same thing. And, even where the early churches differed fundamentally, as did those of Paul from (for instance) that of James in Jerusalem, there is no suggestion that they were not one church. The idea is always there that to be the church one has to participate in the body of Christ, in one sense an invisible body. That is why Christians celebrate the communion of saints, the belief that the church is made up of not just those who are alive and who belong to Christian communities but also those who have died and who are yet to come to life.

Would you make any distinction between the church as Jesus would have envisaged and wanted it and the institutional church we have today?

Catholic...

For many people, the word 'catholic' is a very loaded term. Literally speaking, it just means universal or world-wide; and in that sense all Christians are members of the catholic church. It is, however, a term which has come to be associated with one particular denominational tradition, namely the Roman Catholic church. Roman Catholicism traces its authority to the first apostle Peter, who, it is claimed, became the first bishop or leader of the church in Rome. Because Rome was the capital city of the Roman Empire at that time, the bishop of that city became known as the father of bishops, or the Pope.

The term 'catholic', however, means much more than something which is world-wide or universal. It carries with it also the sense that Christ is fully present whenever two or three Christians gather together to worship and pray. Christ is fully there in the midst of such a gathering, whether it be in a room in the Hebrides or in a big city church.

When you go on holiday and maybe go to a different church, do you feel as much a part of that church as you do your own? If not, why not?

We have now looked at some of the characteristics of the church. What do you think makes a church a church? Is it...
- *The preaching of the Word?*
- *The celebration of the sacraments?*
- *The commitment of the people there in their Christian living, and the way in which the community seeks to serve the world and God?*
- *All of these or something else?*

Oscar Romero was a South American archbishop who was martyred for speaking out on behalf of his people against the injustice of political leaders in the 1970s. For people like Romero, one of the marks of the true church is the mission to which it is called:

> This is the mission entrusted to the church,
> a hard mission:
> to uproot sins from history,
> to uproot sins from the political order,
> to uproot sins from the economy,
> to uproot sins wherever they are
> What a hard task!
> It has to meet conflicts amid so much selfishness,
> so much pride,
> so much vanity,
> so many who have enthroned the reign of sin among us.
>
> The church must suffer for speaking the truth,
> for pointing out sin,
> for uprooting sin.
> No one wants to have a sore spot touched,
> and therefore a society with so many sores twitches

when someone has the courage to touch it
and say: 'You have to treat that'.
  You have to get rid of that.
  Believe in Christ
  Be converted.

Oscar Romero, *The Violence of Love*.

- *Do you feel your local church meets this challenge?*

Given the reality of the church as at once a sinful and sinning, but also a saintly and holy group of people, read the following anonymous poem about the church someone else dreams of:

This is the church of my dreams -
The church of the warm heart,
Of the open mind,
Of the adventurous spirit;
The church that cares,
That heals hurt lives,
That comforts old people,
That challenges youth;
That knows no divisions of culture or class;
No frontiers, geographical or social,
The church that enquires as well as affirms,
That looks forward as well as backward;
The church of the Master,
The church of the people;
High as the ideals of Jesus,
Low as the humblest human;
A working church,
A worshipping church,
A winsome church;
A church that interprets truth in terms of truth;
That inspires courage for this life and hope for the life to come;
A church of courage;
A church of all good people -
The church of the living God.

- *How do you react to this?*
- *Share with one another your dreams for your church.*

At the end of this part of the section on the church, the things we have considered indicate some of the tensions between the church as described in the New Testament, our vision of what the church could be, and what is often expressed in organised churches today.

Given the existence of all these tensions, one of the things which people often hear is that you don't need to go to church in order to be a Christian.

- *Do you believe this to be true?*
- *If it is true, what do you think you might gain or lose in going to church or not going?*

Ministry

How a church is led, where authority is held and how power is exercised are some of the key aspects in a church's internal organisation. These are questions of ministry.

Any group of people over a certain size needs to know where and when it will meet, and for what purpose. A group requires some kind of structure and this includes an understanding of leadership. The church is no different in that respect.

Jesus led his group of disciples, and within the earliest church an inner core seems to have gathered around Peter, James and John. Some, like Judas, had a particular function entrusted to them - in his case to look after the money they held in common (John 12:5-6). From this early group the Christian church came into being.

After Pentecost, the rapid growth of Christian communities called for structures to help maintain the fellowship-life, and to assist in mission to the pagan world. Scholars estimate that within Paul's letters, there are some 80 people named who held leadership roles in the early church. These included teachers (male and female), evangelists, deacons and prophets.

There is a strange contrast between the way ministry is seen in the New Testament, and the way it has developed in the West today. One of the important things to say about ministry is that the New Testament does not suggest one pattern for structuring the way in which the church should minister to others, although it offers some models. Leadership in the early church was fluid, combining formal with informal leadership, and varying from place to place. Over the centuries, ministry has moved from being a function in which everyone shares, to being an office filled by a specially trained and recognised person.

We tend to assume that the recent pattern of full-time ministers is the normal one in

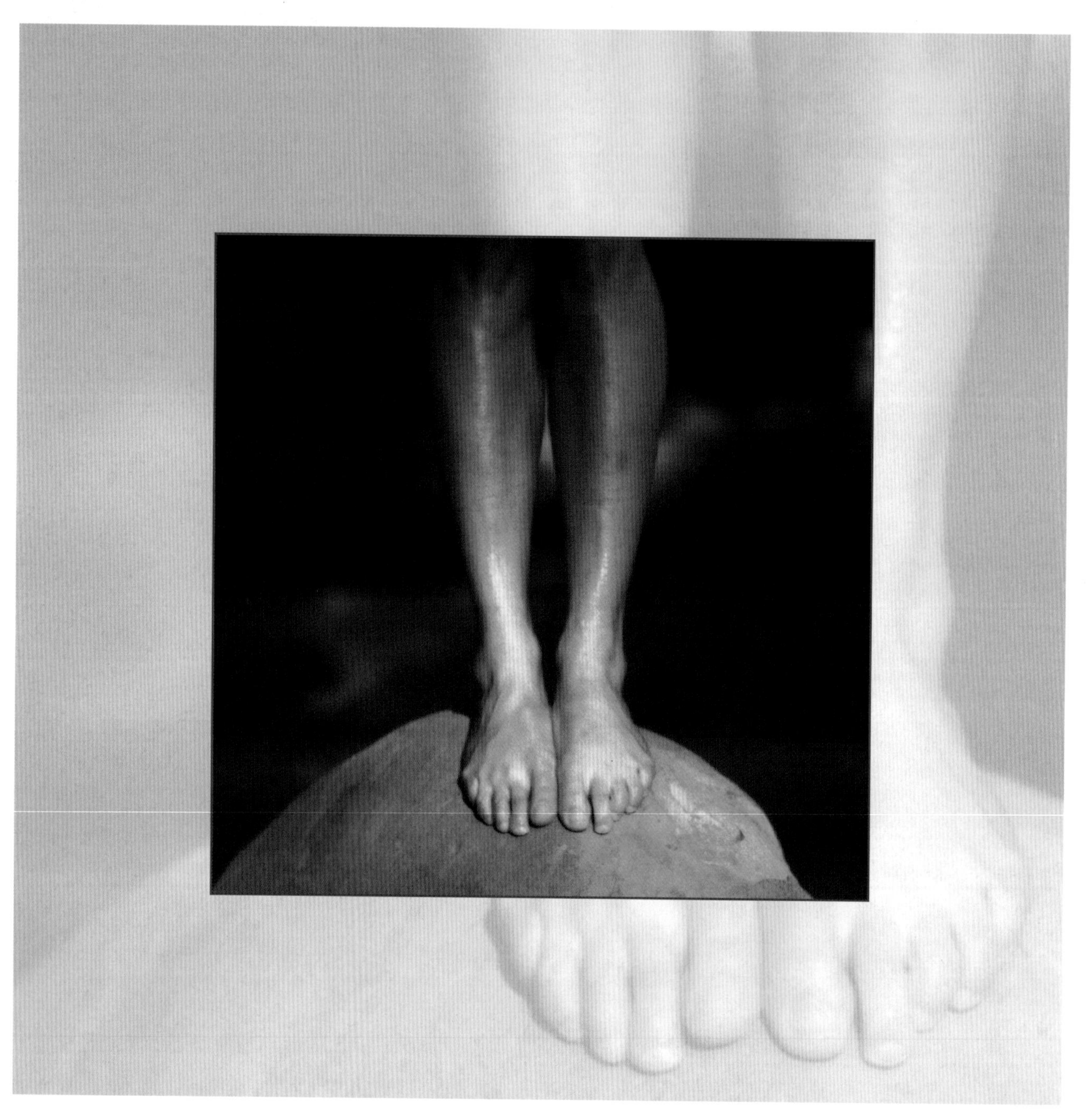

IC
XC

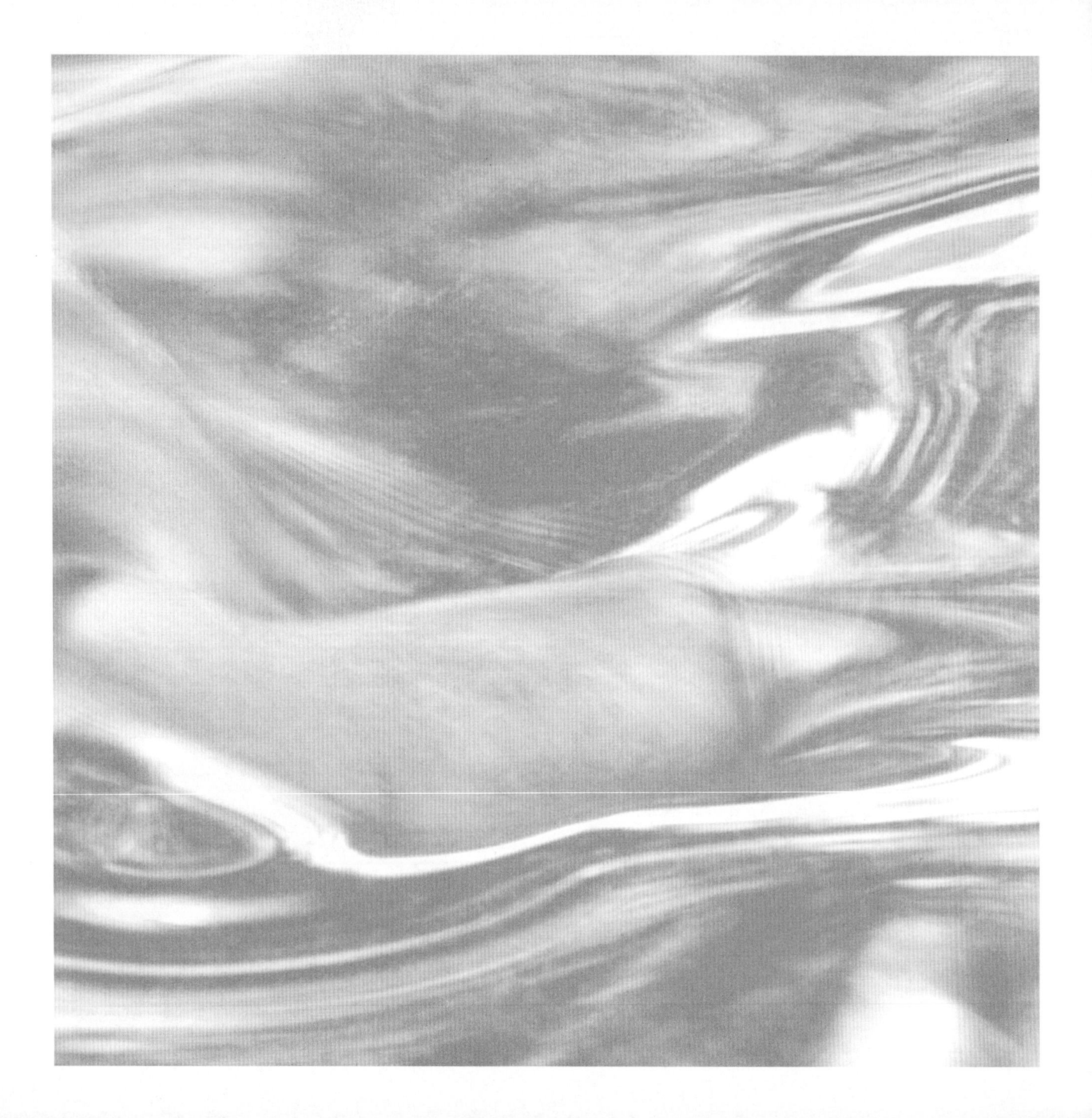

Picture 1

Picture 2

Credit to World Mission
Bangladesh

Credit to NSPCC
(photograph posed by model)

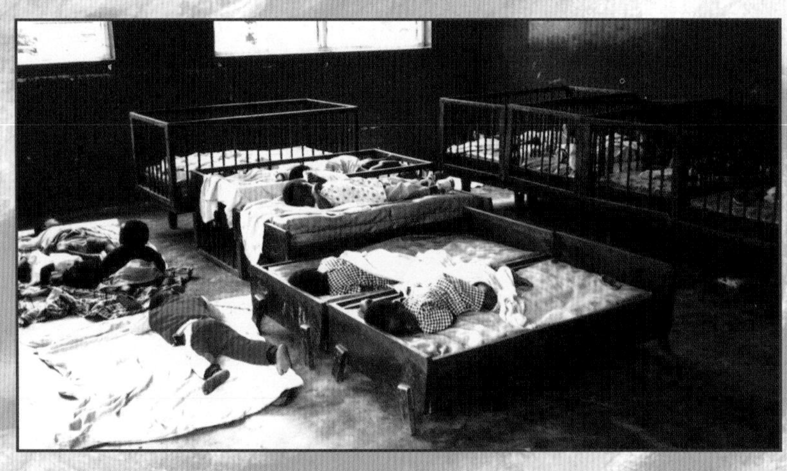
Credit to World Mission
Ghana '91

Christendom. In fact, it was a long time before the full-time ministry developed. In the early centuries, there were many different kinds of ministers: bishops, presbyters, readers, deacons, and several others. Most were unpaid. Even at the Reformation, the minister was seen simply as one among a group of elders (in the Reformed tradition, for instance, the teaching elder among a group of ruling elders). In many parts of the world today, there are thriving Christian denominations with no, or scarcely any, full-time ministers.

Ordination

Ordination is an act - in some churches considered sacramental - recognising an individual as called by God to the task of leadership and the exercising of authority within a particular church community. Thus in a presbyterian situation, elders are ordained in order to exercise spiritual authority through a Kirk Session, the collective meeting of all the elders in a congregation. Within this framework, the minister is a teaching elder within a group of elders, but unlike the others is responsible for his or her actions not to the Kirk Session but to the local Presbytery.

- *Do you feel that ordination is helpful, in that it grants a particular status for the exercising of ministry?*
- *Or do you feel it could be counter-productive in that it highlights the gifts of fewer people within the community?*

Share your thoughts within your group.

Why, then, do we now have 'Ministers', with a capital M? There are six main theories of ministry around today, each of which gives a different answer to that question. Most are not mutually exclusive, and most people will want to hold more than one. The six theories are outlined below.

Share your responses to the questions which follow each statement.

The minister as priest

Some Christians argue that when a Christian congregation meets, its sacraments need to be conducted by someone who has received a special gift from God. This gift is conveyed through succession from the Apostles. By confining the sacraments to those ordained, the church is expressing its belief that all those ordained are able to trace their authority and power to the initial apostles. Some theologies hold that a spiritual power is passed on at ordination.

- *Do you think that it is possible to share in the bread and wine without a minister there to consecrate the elements?*

The minister as authorised teacher

Other Christians see the minister, not as the provider of special grace for the sacraments, but as having special authority for teaching and preaching. They argue that good order and watchfulness against heresy require that certain people need special authorisation, and that only those so authorised can perform such functions. This has been a very important viewpoint within the Scottish tradition which has emphasised the importance of order within worship and discipline within pastoral care.

- *Do you feel that this stress on authorised teaching helps prevent the church from 'falling into false teaching'?*
- *Or does it inhibit others in the Christian community from sharing their knowledge and insights?*

The minister as representative of Christ

Many Christians see the minister as in a special way representing Christ to the congregation, and to the parish. That means that the minister represents 'the church' (the Body of Christ) in a way that lay Christians do not. Hence the significance of chaplains in institutions where lay Christians are present, e.g. hospitals, prisons and industrial places of work. There is also a sense in which the minister is a representative of the wider and worldwide church to the local church community. For that reason, he or she is usually responsible to a level of the church higher than that of the local congregation.

- *Do you feel that there is a benefit in having the church represented by a chaplain, for instance in hospitals, prisons or shopping centres?*

The minister as pastoral leader

Other Christians see the role of the minister as that of leadership of the Christian community. Human groups, they say, need leaders; otherwise they founder. The leader needs to be sensitive to the needs and feelings of the membership, which means that pastoral care and leadership go hand in hand. Part of the minister's leadership might be to pioneer mission, encouraging lay Christians to follow.

- *Many people feel that if they are visited by anyone other than the minister, the visit is not a 'real visit from the church'. What is your reaction to this?*

The minister as enabler

Some Christians see the minister as enabler, responsible for seeing that things are done, but not necessarily for doing them. He or she is responsible for discovering the gifts of others, and seeing that they are equipped to carry out their ministry to one another. Yet it has to be said that many people see the task of ministry as belonging solely to the trained and full-time minister. It is equally true to say that it is not always easy to recognise the particular gifts which people possess and to utilise them in the best way.

- *Do you feel that the gifts of all in your community are being valued sufficiently and used fully?*

'Body' ministry

This view of ministry does away altogether with the idea of 'a minister'. It suggests, on the contrary, that whenever certain individuals are given the role of minister, others find their own ministry inhibited. It holds that just as everyone needs to be ministered to, so everyone has a ministry which they can exercise for the benefit of others: that it is better to discover what gifts God has given everyone towards this end, rather than to appoint particular people to a special 'office' of minister. In this sense it is the whole community, the Body of Christ, which exercises the ministry of that community, rather than placing the responsibility and/or the power with one or two individuals.

One of the significant insights affecting the church in the last few decades is a re-awakening of the Reformation principle called the 'priesthood of all believers'. This states that it is the task and responsibility of all Christians within a church to engage in ministry.

Whilst particular responsibilities are vested in some people, chosen and given authority by the community of the church, it is the challenge of all Christians to share in ministry and service in a local area. This means that the church's ministry cannot rest solely on the ordained: it is only when the community as one body seeks to be true to its calling that the ministry of the church is effective.

- *Do you feel that your skills, abilities and gifts are as well used as they might be within the church community?*
- *Do you feel that you, too, are a minister in your congregation?*

WORSHIP

At several times in their lives, many people have had some kind of an experience of worship. In this section we are going to explore what worship is and why we do it. We will look at something of its history, and elements of both traditional and alternative ways of worshipping God.

Brainstorm in pairs:

- *What comes into your mind when you hear the word 'worship'?*
- *What have been your best/ worst experiences of worship?*

Share your answers with other people in the group.

Did you find any common reasons why a worship service might have been a good or bad experience?

The responses to the first question might not all have been positive. This reflects the tension we often feel between wanting to respond to the presence of God, and sensing that the way we experience worship in church is not fulfilling that urge. A bad worship experience can leave us feeling very far away from God and from one another. It can leave us with feelings of inadequacy, isolation and desperation. Nevertheless, many people still feel the need for a worship experience, regularly or for significant moments - in marriage, in death, for the birth of a child, at festivals such as Christmas or even just on a Sunday morning. So what is it within us that feels this call to worship?

Why worship?

Here are some possible answers to that question:

- ### A response to something beyond

The urge to worship has been described as one of the unique qualities of being human. The word is derived from the old English 'weorthscipe', which means to 'attribute worth'.

Worship is not peculiar to Christians; it is an experience common to people throughout history. It is almost as though our nature demands an expression of wonder at something beyond us, which for Christians is a response to God.

- **We worship because God demands it**

Perhaps a more difficult reason for worshipping is the sense that God demands our worship. We may not be immediately comfortable with this idea, yet just as the people of Israel offered sacrifices to God in the form of animals, Christian worship can be seen as the 'sacrifice' and 'offering' of our lives, words, feelings and prayers to God.

- **We worship because it is our tradition**

The Jewish people worshipped as part and parcel of being in a relationship with God. As Judaism developed, a pattern emerged of regular worship in a recognised sacred space, presided over by priests.

The first Christians worshipped in three ways. The men went to the Temple, where they would have taken part in the sacrifices, and shared in discussions on religion and faith which took place in the outer court (see Acts 2:46 and Acts 21:24-26). They also went to the synagogue, where the service would have started with brief prayers, progressed to a series of Bible readings followed by psalms, continued with a sermon expounding one of the passages, and ended with prayers. Lastly, they would have met with other Christians for breaking of bread and prayer (Acts 2:46 again, and Acts 2:42).

The format of worship which evolved through these early influences has followed the same pattern down through the centuries, although it has been expressed in different ways.

- **Worship is a desire for community**

Jesus told his disciples that whenever two or three were gathered together in his name, he would be there with them. From the start of the Christian church, there was a profound belief that Jesus was particularly present when the community came together to worship. They wanted to be together, to share their sense of joy and celebration at his resurrection, to support and encourage one another in their belief. This reflects our human need to be with one another, especially at key events and moments in our lives.

Having thought through the headings above, read the following statements. (These are from people who were asked to reflect on why they came to worship and what they think happened there.)

'I go to worship because I want to celebrate what God has done for me.'

'Sunday is special... it's God's day... what else should I be doing but remembering God on that day?'

'Life can be a bit of a drag at times... I need my weekly fix... I need to get my batteries charged up so I can face the week.'

'In worship I realise that I am not on my own. I am with a whole community of other people who are with me in my life and that's what worship reminds me of.'

'I go because I feel people will talk about me if I don't.'

'I'm here looking for something... wanting to hear something which might answer some of my questions.'

'It's a good place to catch up with my friends.'

'To provide an occasion for celebration.'

'Worship for me is about honouring God.'

'The service is about reminding me of the old story... telling me again of what God has done.'

'For me, worship is not about me, but about giving me the chance to pray for and think of others who are in need.'

'It's a time to be quiet and silent in my busy life.'

'God speaks to me here... and I listen.'

How do you react to these comments?

Share your feelings in the group.

- *Do any of them speak for you, too?*
- *Could you say why worship is important to you?*

So what is worship?

When we looked at why we worship, we might have been thinking mainly about why we come together for a traditional Sunday worship service.

Look back at the words that people associated with worship. Were these mostly about 'Sunday' worship?

Worship as a whole is much bigger than anything we might experience within the constraints of our Sunday services. We can worship on our own, and we can worship at all times of the day or in any place we choose. We can worship without words and familiar patterns.

Look at the following extract:

> The moon, serene and detached in a cloudless sky... sank earthwards reluctantly, and left them, and mystery once more held field and river.
>
> Then a change began slowly to declare itself. The horizon became clearer, field and tree came into sight, and somehow with a different look; the mystery began to drop away from them. A bird piped suddenly, and was still; and a light breeze sprang up and set the reeds and bulrushes rustling. Rat, who was in the stern of the boat, while Mole sculled, sat up suddenly and listened with a passionate intentness. Mole, who with gentle strokes was just keeping the boat moving while he scanned the banks with care, looked at him with curiosity.
>
> 'It's gone!' sighed the Rat, sinking back in his seat again. 'So beautiful and strange and new! Since it was to end so soon, I almost wish I had never heard it, for it has roused a longing in me that is pain, and nothing seems worthwhile but just to hear that sound once more and go on listening to it forever. No! There it is again!' he cried, alert once more. Entranced, he was silent for a long space, spellbound.
>
> 'Now it passes on and I begin to lose it,' he said presently. 'O, Mole! the beauty of it! The merry bubble and joy, the thin, clear happy call of the distant piping! Such music I never dreamed of, and the call in it is stronger than the music is sweet! Row on Mole, row! For the music and the call must be for us.'
>
> The Mole, greatly wondering, obeyed. 'I hear nothing myself,' he said, 'but the wind playing in the reeds and rushes and osiers'.
>
> The Rat never answered, if indeed he heard. Rapt, transported, trembling, he was possessed in all his senses by this new divine thing that caught up his helpless soul and swung and dangled it, a powerless but happy infant in a strong sustaining grasp.
>
> In silence Mole rowed steadily, and soon they came to a point where the river divided, a long backwater branching off to one side. With a slight movement of his head Rat, who had long dropped the rudder-lines, directed the rower to take the backwater. The creeping tide of light gained and gained, and now they could see the colour of the

flowers that gemmed the water's edge.

'Clearer and nearer still,' cried the Rat joyously. 'Now you must surely hear it! Ah - at last - I see you do!'

Breathless and transfixed, the Mole stopped rowing as the liquid run of that glad piping broke on him like a wave, caught him up and possessed him utterly. He saw the tears on his comrade's cheeks and bowed his head and understood. For a space they hung there, brushed by the purple loosestrife that fringed the bank; then the clear imperious summons that marched hand-in-hand with the intoxicating melody imposed its will on Mole, and mechanically he bent to his oars again. And the light grew steadily stronger, but no birds sang as they were wont to do at the approach of dawn; and but for the heavenly music all was marvellously still.

On either side of them, as they glided onwards, the rich meadow-grass seemed that morning of a freshness and a greenness unsurpassable. Never had they noticed the roses so vivid, the willow-herb so riotous, the meadow-sweet so odorous and pervading.

from *The Wind in the Willows* by Kenneth Grahame

- *What is happening here?*
- *Is worship taking place?*
- *Do you have that same sense - of awe, of wonder, of 'something beyond' - when you take part in Sunday worship?*
- *Have you experienced anything that you would call worship, while not in a worship setting?*

What's going on in worship?

People who create worship are trying to allow space for the expression of the experiences and emotions we have just been thinking about to happen. One of the challenges is that whenever worship takes place, the person or group leading has to be aware of a variety of factors which come into play. For instance we all have different tastes and temperaments; we all use language in different ways. Some people like change and innovation, others the familiar and traditional.

Bearing in mind all these tensions, it is hardly surprising that a worship service is something which can divide members of a congregation. It may even be the very thing which prevents people coming to church, or which causes dispute and disagreement.

However, for many people the occasion and the need to worship God lie at the heart of what it means to be a Christian, so we need to continually re-examine what we do in worship.

In this section we will think of some of the factors which are involved in influencing our own individual approach to worship.

Taste and temperament

How we react to a worship service is affected by whether or not it happens in a way we like - in other words, does it appeal to our taste? We all have different likes and dislikes. Some people love the music of Gregorian Chant and hate Abba, others vice versa. Some like quiet and silence, others noise and activity. But worship must attempt to feed and meet the needs of all in the congregation.

Another factor which affects our response to forms of worship is our temperament. Some of us are private people who want to remain somewhat detached in worship, seeing it as an individual activity, albeit undertaken in the company of other individuals. Some of us are more extrovert and gregarious, and for them, the social dimension of worship is paramount; whether it be meeting old friends or tea and coffee after the service, or just exchanging the peace within the service - though that may range from a handshake to a bearhug!

Meeting the different tastes of people in a congregation is a real challenge for those who lead worship, bearing in mind their different ages, personalities and backgrounds. Some churches try to achieve this by having two or more services in different styles - perhaps a more informal family service, a traditional service, and/or an alternative worship service in the evening.

- *Do you think it is helpful to group the worshipping community differently in this way?*
- *Is it possible for everyone to worship together and have their needs met - or not?*

Tradition

Christian worship developed from drawing on past ways (mostly the Jewish tradition of worship), and on the local culture. It is still developing, given the addition of the culture and experience of contemporary worshippers in every age. The result is that today, for instance, in an Eastern Orthodox Church and a Hebridean Free Church, worship looks very different - but you can see that both have the same roots. Both traditions sing psalms; both bless bread and wine; both pray and preach; but their way of doing these things is rather different.

We are all influenced by traditions in worship. Some are the traditions of generations, while others are the trends of two or three years. Modern trends quickly become traditions themselves, just a little less dusty!

Different traditions have developed in different parts of the church:

- the **Anglican** and **Roman Catholic** branches emphasise the fixed pattern of the worship service (liturgy) and the use of a prayer book
- the **Reformed** branch emphasises the importance of preaching and teaching in worship
- the **Pentecostal** emphasises the expression of the gifts of the Spirit, such as speaking in tongues and words of prophecy
- the **Quaker** emphasises silence.

It can make us feel uncomfortable, but it can also liberate us when we learn that our way of doing things is only one way among many. History demonstrates that there is nothing absolute about forms of worship. Yet people hold very strongly to the traditions involved in their form of worship service because they are a link with the past and their community.

Consider the following story:

> When the guru sat down to worship each evening the ashram cat would get in the way and distract the worshippers. So he ordered the cat to be tied up during worship.
>
> Long after the guru died the cat continued to be tied up during evening worship. And when the cat eventually died, another cat was brought to the ashram so that it could be duly tied up during evening worship.
>
> Centuries later learned essays were written by the guru's disciples on the essential role of a cat in all properly conducted worship.
>
> Anon

- *What do you feel that this story says about tradition in worship?*
- *How much of the worship you experience is shaped by a feeling of 'it's always been done this way', in your opinion?*
- *What are the core elements of your tradition that you wouldn't want to lose?*

*You may find it helpful at this point to look at the Further Reading section on **page 161**, on the development and history of worship.*

Culture

One of the insights from the cat story is that things which once made sense (in the culture and context in which they started) may remain long after their original sense and meaning has been lost. For instance, the reason why ministers wear black is that in the sixteenth century, black robes were formally accepted as the appropiate clothing for those in the teaching professions. At that time, wearing black helped to make ministers appear *less* priestly and distant from the people they ministered to - unlike contemporary priests who tended to be quite elaborately dressed in more distinctive clothing - because it conformed to a recognisable and common dress-code. Dressing as teachers made ministers relevant to the society of the time. Today, however, the minister is *identified* by being dressed in black, particularly in the traditional sixteenth century robes. The very garb which was originally so 'normalising' now seems largely irrelevant and at times a bit of a caricature.

In Scotland it can also be said that the act of worship reflects a very narrow band of Scottish cultural life. For example there is still a large emphasis on the verbal rather than the visual; on using formal modes of expression rather than colloquial language or dialect. There is still an emphasis on formal dress and behaviour rather than the kind of informality now more common in other forms of social interaction.

Many people today are alienated from attending worship because they feel that it is foreign to their own culture and upbringing.

Share with one another in small groups:

- *Do you feel that the worship in your own area is reflective of the people, the culture and the time in which you are living?*
- *If not, why not?*

We have considered culture here mostly in a local sense; but we should also remember that we can now also look on ourselves as members of a 'global village'. Recently, in Africa and India, amongst other places, Christians have been rediscovering more locally relevant ways of worshipping, through music, song, prayer and praise which come from their own culture. Their experiences, in turn, can enrich our worship.

Language

The language and words used in the service are important factors in worship. The language has to be comprehensible and accessible, or else the worship-leader and those involved in presenting worship are failing to communicate with the congregation. For this reason, many ancient hymns and prayers - e.g. the Lord's Prayer - are being rewritten today, and new ones composed whose language and thought forms are more contemporary and easily understood. There is an increased awareness that the language we use in worship must be sensitive to the society in which that worship takes place. For instance, in a church where there are many single people, is it appropriate to refer to the church community as a 'family'? There has been much debate too concerning the introduction of 'inclusive' language into formal worship; many people think that the language of religion is often frankly 'sexist' while others think that the language of the church should stand apart from this kind of modern 'improvement'.

- *Make a list of words you hear in worship or in a church setting which you don't hear used outside.*
- *Do you think it is necessarily a problem that we have at times a separate 'religious' language?*
- *How do you think people feel if they don't know this 'in' language?*
- *What can we do about this?*

Visual aspects of worship

From the earliest days of religious worship, people have been sensitive to the ways in which objects and symbols, pictures and paintings can help people to gain a sense of worship and to encounter the divine. Protestants have always struggled with the use of such objects in worship, fearing that they might lead to the veneration of what the Bible calls 'graven images' and 'idols'. By that is meant any physical object which represents God; including statues, paintings and stained glass depicting Jesus and/or God. Nevertheless, the last century has witnessed a gradual increase in the use of the visual within a very word-dominated Protestant worship practice. The reasons for this are numerous; but by and large, the increase reflects a greater emphasis placed on the visual within wider culture and society, in an age where ideas and messages are no longer communicated by words alone, but also through pictures, music and movement.

Think about the ways in which we use the buildings we worship in, and whether or not they assist our worship lives.

- *Do we use pictures, candles, objects (e.g. stones), in our worship?*
- *Would you feel comfortable with the use of such things in a worship service?*

Share your answers with others in your group.

Order of service

Christian worship is rarely just a haphazard putting-together of ingredients. It's usually the expression of a feeling that the structure must make sense, and that within it things must be 'done properly'. This deliberate structuring is often referred to as 'order'.

The only explicit teaching we have on worship order is in 1 Corinthians 14:26ff, where Paul's concern is for orderliness - that where spontaneous outbursts have become perhaps excessive, there should be an attempt to control their expression. However, the instructions he gives - about one person bringing a hymn, another a revelation, or where one person might speak in tongues and another interpret this - show that worship should arise out of the life of the Christian community, wherever it happens to be in its pilgrimage. Worship is to be expressed by the community, out of the life of that community under the inspiration of the Spirit, for the building up of the Body of Christ in that place, and for the glory of God.

Paul reminds us that there is continual tension between the need for order and yet for flexibility within the worship service; for variety and yet familiarity. In his letters to the church in Corinth he talks of God as a God of order, not disorder. See 1 Corinthians 14:26-33.

Think back to the last time you were in church or attended a worship service.

- *Can you remember the order of the service?*
- *Try to write this down.*

How did you get on?

Worship in many Protestant church services follows a specific pattern:

Us to God
Call to worship - Focusing on our need to worship God and the reasons why we are there.
Adoration - Being aware of the presence of God and giving praise to God as Creator, involved in our world and in our lives.
Invocation - Asking to become more aware of the presence of God.
Confession - Presenting where we have fallen short in our relationship with God and with one another.
Supplication - Being sorry and asking forgiveness.
Assurance of forgiveness - Being assured of God's love and faithfulness to us despite what we have done or might do.

God to us
God speaks to us through the readings and the preaching of the Word.
Readings - often there are two or three reflecting the Old Testament, a letter from the New Testament and one of the four Gospels.
Sermons - a means by which the Word which has been read is illuminated and addressed to the congregation. The preacher shares not only his or her own views but also the Word as God communicates it to the congregation. Historically this was viewed as being of such importance in the Reformed tradition that sermons could sometimes go on for hours - they tend to be shorter today!

Our response to God
Offering - making an offering of the whole of our lives as well as our material gifts.
Intercession and petition - through prayer, seeking help for others and ourselves.
Thanksgiving - through music and prayer, giving thanks to God for the Word that has been received.
Blessing and sending forth - receiving the blessing and being sent out to be the people of God.

Where the sacrament of communion is celebrated, the communion often starts just after the offering has been received.

Have a look at this service order.
- *Do you sense the pattern which is there?*
- *How does it relate to your normal Sunday experience?*
- *Does this structure address the needs of different kinds of worshippers?*
- *Does it allow space for people to be able to worship in their own ways?*
- *Or might this pattern not suit everyone?*

How do you feel about worship?

Read the following statements about worship. How far do you agree or disagree with each one?

Strongly Agree (4) Agree (3) Disagree (2) Strongly disagree (1)

1. A minister or recognised lay leader is needed to conduct the service.
2. There should normally be a sermon.
3. A printed order of service is helpful.
4. Laughter, chatter and applause are inappropriate in worship.
5. Lots of different instruments should be used to accompany the singing.
6. Written parts for people to say together are essential.
7. It is important to have times of silence.
8. Visual stimulation (e.g. posters, banners, icons, objects, candles) is an aid to worship.
9. Prayers for the current problems of the world should always be included.
10. Scripture, songs and choruses are an integral part of worship.

What, in your opinion, are the most important elements of a worship service? What elements do you think must be present in order to for you to feel that you are worshipping?

Final thoughts

Times of worship are, potentially, occasions when we can encounter and meet God in a new and at times uncomfortable way. Some people would say that to enter worship to meet God is a dangerous and unsettling event. Ancient Celtic and Orthodox Christian tradition considers that in worship we wait for the presence of God to direct and fill our lives. This is the reason why some would argue that worship has to be spontaneous and must enable the Holy Spirit to be present.

Another dimension not to be forgotten is that we cannot truly worship without responding to God in all parts of our lives; our response shows through the choices we make about the way in which we treat others. Worship takes place not just in the sanctuary but in the street. A key element of Christian worship has always been offering our whole life to God.

- *Do you feel that the worship of which you are a part reflects this?*

Read the following extract:

> In Brazil I sat with a woman - a mother - on a bare hillside. She and her people have lost almost all of their land. Nothing would grow on this woman's hillside. There was one dirty stream at this bottom of the hill with a few fish, otherwise there was nothing to eat. Two yards in front of where we sat was a small circle of wooden crosses. It was where she buried her children, beneath the dust. She had no food or medicine to keep them alive.
>
> The parable of the sheep and the goats suggests that God is like that woman; that when I think of God, I should think of praying and turning to someone like her. What should I offer such a God when I come to worship? And what should I expect such a God to do for me when I am frightened and in trouble? And when I pray, what should I say to such a God, this woman who has nothing at all?
>
> I sat beside her as part of a world which crucifies and shuts her out - that refuses to stretch out its hand to feed her and clothe her and visit her, or comfort her children. Yet, like the crucified, her arms are open wide in welcome. She greets me as a friend. She offers to share what she has, and thanks me for coming.
>
> This is the Advent God who came in Jesus of Nazareth. This is Emmanuel, God with us, forever empty and forever full - who comes and comes again in the poorest of the poor.
>
> Michael Taylor

- *How would you worship with this woman?*

SACRAMENTS

and other services

In this section we will look at the sacraments and special services of the Church. Before we do that we will spend some time thinking about why sacraments, or moments which we call sacramental, are important for us. Why should rituals, our use of symbols, our need for security and identity matter in our worship? Why should we give such special status to one or two specific acts of worship? How do these acts relate to the key moments we experience in our life?

Ritual

Ritual plays an important part in our society. Ritual begins early. Large numbers of small children insist on a ritual, for instance at bedtime. The story has to be read a certain way, the right teddy tucked in the proper place. Even the right words or gestures should be used - a kiss for teddy, a kiss for dolly, then a kiss for the child; and the child may be quite upset if it isn't done right, often making the parent come back and do it again. Each family will have elements of daily life enshrouded with ritual. Who sits where at the meal-table; what time people go to bed; which chair is whose in the front room; who gets the bedtime drinks.

Worship is a ritual. At the same time each week, people meet and go through the same procedure. They do the right things almost instinctively at the right moments - standing for hymns, head-bowing for prayers, sitting back for the sermon. They know the little signals which indicate what's about to happen - the change in the minister's tone which suggests that he or she is about to begin the sermon. Their built-in clocks tell them what stage the ritual should have reached by what time, and they become uneasy if it doesn't seem to be going according to anticipation. Even the language is ritualised. The words might vary from week to week, but they are in a form that only ever belongs to this context. We even know the words that indicate that a prayer is about to end.

Think about your own life. Take an ordinary day and think about whether there are any things which you do which you might call rituals.

Share your thoughts about rituals with others in your group.

- *Do you think that doing things in a particular pattern in worship lessens their impact*
- *Or might it increase their impact?*

So what do all these rituals do for us? Here are some suggestions:

Security

One of the things rituals can do is help us to feel secure. Rituals make the world a safe place. They reassure us. The more stress and rapid change we undergo in one part of our lives, the more we ritualise the other parts, to give us a secure base. This was perhaps especially the case for the first Christians. They were living in very uncertain times. They had no real security - they did not belong, indeed were told not to belong to the world.

Celebrating a sacrament such as communion helps us to focus on an action which has taken place across the years and generations. It is a familiar act. This means that we can, to some extent, be comfortable with the familiarity. It's rather like putting on a favourite item of clothing or even something worn by a grandparent. The sacraments link us with the origins of our tradition but also help us to remember where we have come from as individuals. For many people, the celebration of communion is a most intimate reminder of childhood church involvement. This can be both positive and negative. Because the particular way in which a sacrament is celebrated is important to people, changes in that form can be very upsetting.

- *How easy do you find it if changes in worship are introduced in your church?*

Identity

In our society, the nearest parallel to worship is probably the ritual of the football ground. It has its chants and songs, its own strange language, its predictable pattern of activity. As with worship, the content is different from week to week - no two football games are identical - but each occasion is fundamentally like the last.

Football ritual is all about identity. Through it, people identify with the team and make themselves part of it. For that hour and half, they identify totally with its fortunes, and the excitement reinforces an identity which continues all week. Not a few people live for their team, its games being the highlight of the week.

Christian worship is also an identity ritual, though sadly seldom one with the same intensity as that of the football stadium. It, too, is about feeling you belong and knowing what you are. For churchgoers, the ritual of church-going performs many of the same functions. If being a 'church member' is an important part of my self-image - the identity I project to myself and others - simple attendance re-enforces it. I may keep on going, even though I don't enjoy it much at all (in fact, I might even think I shouldn't enjoy it). Take it away, and I shall be lost.

Baptism and confirmation play the same sacramental role in confirming our identity and association as a member of the Christian community. They give us a sense of belonging. The ritual of baptism also helps to underline our own sense of belonging whenever anyone else joins the community.

Symbol

Rituals can work as symbols. Symbols represent deeply rooted aspects of society. The flag, for instance, is a symbol of nationhood. As such, it takes on special significance. For an American, the Stars and Stripes aren't just decorations on a piece of cloth representing America, they are more than that. Whenever someone burns or destroys an American flag it is almost as if they are destroying part of what it means to be American.

To fly the Saltire in Scotland is to assert something important about the people who fly it. The fact that the Saltire can be seen everywhere in Scotland, but that in England, the British Union Jack rather than the English cross of St George is widely flown, tells you something about the contrasting sense of national identity between the two nations. For the early Jews, the Temple had more than a superficial religious significance. It was the most important symbol of who and what they were, as the nation chosen by God. For that reason the only wall which remains from the original Temple has huge spiritual significance for Jews to this day.

We use symbols a great deal in our sacraments because they perform the function of illustrating something not always easily expressed in words. The objects we use as symbols enable us to allow our imagination to work in a way which is freer and more open to the Spirit than words might be.

Now we come to the idea and understanding of sacrament which is closely linked to that of ritual and symbol.

Look at these symbols. What messages do they give to you?

- *Think about symbols that you see around you.*
- *Are symbols always positive?*

The word 'sacrament' comes from the Latin 'sacramentum' - originally an oath taken by soldiers joining a Roman legion.

In the religious sense a sacrament is a religious act which is 'an outward and visible sign of an inward and spiritual grace'. These are difficult words, but basically mean something which points to God. Sacraments have a visible or external element like water or wine, and an invisible or internal part which is the Holy Spirit working through the physical water or bread and wine.

In the Roman Catholic and Orthodox traditions there are the following seven sacraments: baptism, the Eucharist, confirmation, matrimony, penance, holy orders (ordination), and extreme unction (the sacrament of healing).

For most Protestants there are only two: baptism, and the Eucharist. These are the sacraments explicitly described in Scripture. However, some Reformers debated as to whether ordination was a sacrament, notably Calvin, who in some of his writings was in favour of it being so described.

Sacraments are therefore symbolic events, moments and movements in the life of the church. They are a means through which God comes close. Symbols are all around us. We use our bodies to express what we mean by gesture and mannerisms. We all know what a handshake symbolises - welcome and acceptance. For Christians the sacraments help to communicate our deepest religious feelings and thoughts in an act which points to God.

The sacraments also help to mark out key events in someone's life, e.g. entry into the church is marked as an adult or child by baptism.

We will now look at the sacraments of baptism and communion.

Baptism and initiation

Traditionally, the first sacrament which many people experience in the church is that of baptism. It is the act of introduction or initiation through which people are welcomed into a Christian community. Infant baptism has been the traditional practice; although some Christians, including Baptists, argue that a person should be baptised only when he or she is old enough to be able to say that they believe in Jesus, so that usually only adults are baptised.

Christian baptism originates from various Jewish practices. We read in parts of the New Testament that the practice of immersing in or sprinkling with water soon became recognised as the way into belonging to the Christian community. The New Testament says various things about baptism but it is clear that the image of water was used to convey different messages to those welcomed into the church.

Cleansing:

Water cleanses and so there is an emphasis on baptism as something which makes the person clean and pure in body and spirit. Water is a powerful symbol suggesting refreshment, cleansing and newness of life.

Baptism is also an opportunity to remember God's activity since the beginning of time. It provides an occasion for the new member to renounce everything bad in their lives and to take on board the challenges of becoming a disciple of Jesus.

Participation:

One of the oldest baptism images is that through baptism all that is wrong in our lives dies and we symbolically take part in Jesus' death and resurrection by being 'drowned' and 'raised through the water'. This is more understandable when the body is fully immersed but it still carries a certain power when there is no full immersion. So the idea of newness - new life, new creation and new beginning - is emphasised. See Romans 6:3-6.

Gift of the Holy Spirit:

Closely related to baptism from the earliest times was the sense and belief that the Holy Spirit was especially associated with it (see Acts 8:14ff). In former times people were given new clothes to indicate that their baptism service marked a new beginning. In many countries today the newly baptised are given a candle to show the light that has come into their lives. Indeed, an old Celtic description of baptism is to call the service the 'enlightening'.

Welcoming:

Baptism is a sacrament in that, through the outward sign of water, we are shown that a person belongs to God. It is the community's act of welcoming a new member into their company. It is not however an end in itself, though it is never repeated because it is an act of initiation.

Look at these words from the baptism service. Can you see here the elements we have talked about?

Statement

The minister says:

Christ is present with us in the sacrament;
it is he himself who baptizes us,
and by the Spirit of Pentecost
he brings us into his Church.

Baptism is the sign of dying to sin
and rising to new life in Christ.

By water and the Holy Spirit,
God claims us as his own,
washes us from sin,
and sets us free from the power of death.
Here we know
that we are made one with Christ
crucified and risen,
members of his body,
called to share his ministry in the world.

In this sacrament
the love of God is offered to each one of us.
Though we cannot understand or explain it,
we are called to accept that love
with the openness and trust of a child.
In baptism,
N... is assured
of the love that God has for her,
and the sign and seal of the Holy Spirit
is placed upon her.

Declaration

For each child, the minister says such words as:

N…,
for you Jesus Christ came into the world:
for you he lived and showed God's love;
for you he suffered the darkness of Calvary
and cried at the last, 'It is accomplished';
for you he triumphed over death
and rose in newness of life;
for you he ascended to reign at God's right hand.
All this he did for you, N…,
though you do not know it yet.
And so the word of Scripture is fulfilled:
'We love because God loved us first'.

Book of Common Order of the Church of Scotland

Traditionally many people, even if they have had little connection with the church, have brought their children to be baptised. This was encouraged by former teachings suggesting that an unbaptised child had no hope of eternal life. Baptism was also traditionally important because it highlighted the desire within us to give thanks for the birth of a child and to have the community recognise that birth. More recently, there have been suggestions that a civic naming ceremony should be offered to those of no formal religious faith, so that a child might be ritually named and welcomed into the wider community.

- *Share your feelings about this idea. Does the ritual of baptism make people feel that they are accepted and belong?*

The way in which we are welcomed and included into the Christian community has changed over the years. There are many more people now who come to church who were not baptised as infants and this number is likely to increase over the next few decades. There are many more who find it difficult to belong to one particular religious community.

- *Do we need to create a new ritual to meet the needs of these people?*
- *Do you think we need an act of baptism to make people feel they belong?*

Confirmation

In the early church when someone was baptised they were immediately confirmed in membership through being anointed with oil, indicating the gift of the Holy Spirit. The act of confirmation also involved a 'laying on of hands', as a blessing for the baptised person. There was a sense that from this point onward he or she had become an 'ambassador' for Christ.

For various historical reasons by the fifth century, confirmation was no longer directly connected with baptism. Over time, the custom arose where a child's baptism was confirmed when they were old enough to be able to make the vow of membership and assent to belief themselves.

In many churches confirmation has remained a sacrament. It is an opportunity for children and adults to own and profess the faith into which they may have been baptised when younger. In practice, being confirmed meant that a person could then receive the sacrament of communion. Many churches hold enquiry or membership classes, providing interested individuals with an opportunity to think about some of the issues of faith that this book is attempting to tackle.

The other important element of confirmation is that it enables public profession of a faith which, up until that moment, might have been a private belief. In most services candidates are asked to say the words of a creed, usually the Apostles' Creed, and to take certain vows. Attempts have been made more recently to update the language of the traditional creeds.

Look at both the creed and confirmation vows included in the Further Reading section, ***pp 165****. Share with one another concerns or questions which you might have about them.*

- *Do you feel that the more modern statement of faith speaks to you more than the traditional creed?*
- *Do you think it is important that there are creeds or statements which you can say together with others?*

Communion or Eucharist

The sacrament of communion or Eucharist (thanksgiving) is for many people the most important element within Christian worship. Many denominations hold weekly and sometimes daily sacraments, although the Church of Scotland holds more infrequent celebrations.

Central to the communion is the Last Supper, which Jesus shared with his disciples in the

Upper Room. Its roots are in the Jewish ritual meal. At the start of this meal, God was given thanks as bread was passed round and at the end, a cup of blessing was shared and God was called upon to be present.

Read the following extract:

> One of the many memories that remain vivid in my mind from the days when I used to teach at Union Theological Seminary, New York, is an occasion when my wife and I were dinner guests of the well-known Jewish scholar, Abraham Joshua Heschel, and his wife, in their apartment on Riverside Drive. It was the eve of the Sabbath. At the beginning of the meal, our host took a small loaf of bread into his hands, and said over it a brief prayer, called in Hebrew a *beraka*, a word which can mean 'blessing' or 'thanksgiving'. It ran: 'Blessed are you, Lord God of the universe, you bring forth bread from the earth'. The host then broke the bread, took a piece himself and distributed pieces to those who were gathered round the table. At the end of the meal, as I remember, there were more extended thanksgivings. The host took a cup of wine (the 'cup of blessing', Paul calls it), and said over it a similar *beraka*: 'Blessed are you, Lord God of the universe, you create the fruit of the vine'. He then passed the cup round the guests.
>
> The scene just described could hardly fail to remind a Christian of Jesus' last meal with his disciples on the night before he died. It is quite possible that he used much the same prayers at the Last Supper as I was now hearing from Abraham Heschel. So in the Heschel apartment I had a vivid sense of that Last Supper at which was instituted the Lord's Supper or eucharist, a word which itself means 'thanksgiving'.
>
> from *A Guide to the Sacrament* by John Macquarrie

Every time Jesus ate and drank with his friends, this simple act was carried out. What was significant was that on the occasion before he was handed over to the authorities, Jesus gave the meal a particular resonance. Whenever his followers carried out this simple act they were to do so remembering him. Yet at the heart of it were the ordinary symbols of bread, which filled the body, and wine, which gave warmth, joy and welcome.

- *How important for you is the act of sharing a meal in the company of friends?*
- *What aspect of the act do you feel is present when Christians share the communion meal?*

Read the poem below.

Bread, wine and gentleness

Be gentle
When you
touch bread.
Let it not lie
uncared for,
unwanted:
So often bread
Is taken for granted.
There is such beauty
In bread,
Beauty of sun and soil,
Beauty of patient toil.
Wind and rain have caressed it,
Christ often blessed it.
Be gentle
When you touch bread.

Be loving
When you
drink wine.
So freely received
and joyfully shared
In the spirit of him
who cared.
Warm as a flowing river,
Shining and clear
As the sun.
Deep as the soil
Of human toil.
The winds and rain caressed it.
Christ often blessed it.
Be loving
When you drink wine.

Anon

- *How do you feel about the bread and wine? What do they symbolise for you?*
- *Look at these pictures of bread and wine. What do they say to you?*

The bread and wine, for Christians, symbolise the body and blood of Jesus. One of the sharpest disputes dividing the churches down through history concerns how the bread and wine become the body and blood of Jesus. What is not in dispute is the real sense, from the earliest times, that when the community gathers together to remember Jesus and break bread and share wine, that Jesus is especially present in the company. There are numerous instances which reflect this in the New Testament but one of the most famous is the story of the Emmaus Road: see Luke 24:13-33.

The meal is known to some denominations including Roman Catholics as the Mass. The word 'Mass' comes from the final words of the Latin service, '*ite missa est*' which roughly translated means 'go, ye are sent out'. It is also known as the Eucharist to many Episcopalians and Anglicans and as the Communion or the Lord's Supper to Presbyterians.

Many images and symbolic understandings are associated with the sacrament of communion, but chief amongst them is the sense that the church becomes a real and true community when it is mysteriously united to Jesus in this act. More than a re-enactment and more than a memorial, it is a mystery.

In the actual communion service the central importance of the Last Supper is underlined when the story is re-read for the worshipping community. A further important element is that of thanksgiving. In the prayer before communion, God is thanked for all activities since creation, centring on the life, death and resurrection of Jesus. God is called on to be present in and through the gifts of bread and wine, placed on the table or altar. You will note the clear overtones of sacrifice - for some there is a close relationship between the communion service and the Jewish celebration of the time of Passover, when God protected the people of Israel as they prepared to leave Egypt.

The early church emphasised the celebratory aspect of communion.

- *In your own experience does the celebration of communion today capture the sense of joy at Christ's resurrection?*

One of the major issues for church people today concerns who should or should not receive the bread and wine. We have highlighted above and elsewhere the way in which membership of and belonging to the church is changing. It is perfectly possible that a child who comes every Sunday to church and yet is not baptised is barred from taking the bread and wine whilst someone who comes infrequently but is a 'member' receives the elements. What does this say about the sacrament of communion? Many ministers at the start of their services highlight the fact that the Lord's Table is open to any, to those 'who love the Lord'. Yet there are also scriptural injunctions about eating and drinking the bread and wine carelessly. As part of the service many ministers still include words from I Corinthians 11:27-29:

> Whoever, therefore, eats the bread or drinks the cup of the Lord in an unworthy manner will be answerable for the body and blood of the Lord. Examine yourselves, and only then eat of the bread and drink of the cup. For all who eat and drink without discerning the body, eat and drink judgement against themselves.

Indeed, at one point in history many Scottish churches literally fenced off the Communion Table with something reminiscent of an altar rail. People could only receive the sacrament when they had passed 'the Test'. This was usually a recital of the Lord's Prayer, the Creed and the Catechism, after which they were given small tokens which they presented on the next Sunday to the elders. These tokens later became the communion cards which survive to this day in many Scottish parishes.

Share your feelings on who should be allowed to share at the Table.

Marriage

One of the most frequent occasions when many people attend church, perhaps as often as baptism, is to go to a wedding. It is not surprising that the churches developed an act (for some a sacrament because it is related to the desire to continue humanity) in order to recognise the bonding or pairing of one individual to another. Marriage is a key moment in the life of individuals and so the church recognises this in the presence of others by blessing their union. Yet in Scotland after the Reformation, because it had not been the custom for marriages to be celebrated in church, the practice was largely shunned. During the medieval period, certainly in Scotland, you were simply married by consent and recognition. The church was not involved.

By the middle of the nineteenth century it had become the custom for marriages to be solemnised in the home or at the hotel where the reception was to be held. More and more people, however, wished to be married in church and this was in part influenced by happenings south of the Border. Today many people, with little formal religious involvement, still choose to be married in churches.

In the service the church seeks to underline the belief that marriage is still fundamental for the fabric of society, not least for the creation of children and the enjoyment of a sexual relationship. This is increasingly a position under challenge, given that some 65 percent of couples live together before their wedding day. The church in the marriage service tries to emphasise the selfless nature of the love a couple ought to have for one another, often relating this to the love of Christ. That is why 1 Corinthians 13: 'Love is not proud ...etc.' is often used. There is recognition that this is a key point in the life of the couple and that it is important for the community. The life-long commitment involved in such an undertaking is emphasised and the minister or priest blesses the couple.

We have noted that not all churches describe marriage as a sacrament.

- *Do you feel that when you watch or are part of a marriage service there is a sense of God's special presence rather like at communion or baptism?*

Society has changed considerably, divorces are becoming increasingly common and the existence of same sex relationships is not uncommon. Relationships break up and where children are involved there can be hurt and recrimination.

Look at the following rituals, created to allow gay and lesbian people to have a commitment ceremony:

1. We have gathered together today to acknowledge the love which has brought N and N together as being from God and to ask God's blessing upon them as they live together in company with each other. We also seek to give them support as their friends and as members of the Body of Christ, the church, and to strive for their good now in our prayers and in our future care and concern.

Each friend repeats the following: In the presence of God and God's people, I, N, declare my love for you, N, and seek God's blessing on our friendship. I will continue to love you, care for you, and consider you before my own needs, in good times and through periods of difficulty. I will rejoice when you are happy and grieve when you suffer. I will share your interests and hopes for the future. I will try to understand you even when I do not agree with you. I will help you to be your true self - the person God wishes you to be. In all this I ask God's help, now and in the days to come. In the name of Jesus Christ. Amen.

(Hazel Barkham)

2. N and N, you are about to make a solemn promise. Do you believe God has called you to live together in love?

We do believe.

Do you promise to be loyal to each other, never allowing any other relationship to come before the one you are now to affirm?

We do promise.

Will you give yourselves wholeheartedly and without reserve?

We will.

Will you, under God, recognise each other's freedom to grow as individuals and allow each other time and space to do so?

We will.

Will you do all in your power to make your life together a witness to the love of God in the world?

We will.

To each partner in turn: N, will you give yourself wholly to N, sharing your love and your life, your wholeness and your brokenness, your joys and sorrows, your health and sickness, your riches and poverty, your success and failure?

I will.

(Jim Cotter)

3. Today we pledge ourselves to a commitment in love. Our commitment to each other comes from a belief that God is with us. In our union we would seek to offer companionship to each other in

every area of our life together. We would seek to bear fruit through our relationship, in the way it touches our family, our friends and those around us.

Daring to Speak Love's Name, a Gay and Lesbian Prayer Book edited by Dr Elizabeth Stuart

- *Do you feel that the church needs to recognise (or should be involved in recognising) how the way people relate to one another is changing?*

Confession

One of the oldest Christian sacraments is known as confession. Although the Presbyterian tradition does not call confession sacramental, it still plays an important part in the prayer life of the community. It seems to be part of our nature that we fall out of relationship with other people, frequently with those who matter most to us. The process of restoring that relationship, of making peace, of healing the hurt between two people, lies at the heart of confession. Christians would say that they have fallen short in their relationship with God, through what they have done, as well as through things they have not done, deliberately or not. For this reason, Christians believe in the need to restore that relationship with God and that the first act of this restoration is to say sorry and seek forgiveness. It is in so doing that we are reconciled with God.

Some traditions believe that through the words of forgiveness uttered by a priest the forgiving grace of God is communicated to the person seeking forgiveness. For this reason confession has been called 'the sacrament of reconciliation'. It gives the person who is sorry (penitent) an opportunity for a fresh start. Some traditions have a system whereby sin is confessed in private to a priest-confessor who assists in finding ways to restore relationship. Other traditions use corporate prayer so that there is a sense in which the community is seeking and receiving forgiveness together.

Arguably, modern society often does not provide people with the opportunity to feel valued and accepted for who and what they are. People need to have opportunities to unburden themselves of guilt they may feel, or which they may be made to feel for things they have done. Confession, in whatever form, provides one such opportunity. Indeed, Scripture emphasises the importance of restoring our relationship with others, e.g. Luke 6:41-42.

Being able to recognise where you went wrong enables people to make a new start, to wipe the slate clean, to begin again. It helps us to be truthful with ourselves, to see ourselves as others see us. It is also through confession that the Holy Spirit works to deepen our relationship with God, even during times of pain.

- *In your own experience are there enough opportunities for people to reflect on what has gone wrong in their lives?*
- *Do you feel that the church helps people in this regard or does it just make them feel more hopeless and guilty?*
- *Could we create more meaningful ways in a church service to allow us to say sorry - both individually or together?*

Healing

Closely related to confession are the scriptural commands to pray for and look after those who are sick, ill or dying, as in James 5:14-15. The ministry of Jesus is dominated by his physical healing, acceptance and inclusion of those who had been rejected, hurt or driven to the edge. Some traditions consider that healing is a sacrament. Frequently this sacrament, also known as the anointing of the sick, is associated with those who are seriously ill. As a consequence, the term 'last rites' is often associated with it. During the sacrament of healing, the individual confesses their sin, receives the communion and is blessed by the priest. Importantly too the sacrament includes the laying on of hands by the priest. In this area there is resonance with services of healing which have become increasingly common in many churches today. Through the laying on of hands the person ministering is following in the line of Christ whose ministry was marked by intimate physical gestures (see Mark 8:22ff).

The early church carried on the practice of healing the sick and those who were hurt. Although such practices died out they have become more common in the 20th century, associated as they are with the charismatic and Pentecostal movements.

The ministry of healing is a very sensitive area. The church does not claim that every time someone receives the laying on of hands they will be physically healed. Rather, through the sacrament of healing, the Holy Spirit is enabled to work in the person who is suffering.

How comfortable are you with stories of healing?

- *Have you any experience of a service of healing? What was your response to it?*
- *Can you imagine any way for a healing ritual to be incorporated into our Church's worship?*

The last of the seven sacraments is ordination: this is discussed in the Church and Ministry section on **page 75**.

We talked earlier about what a sacrament is, and why it is so important in developing a community's relationship with God. One of the things the sacraments do is to break down the barriers between the visible and the invisible. Through the sacraments, people feel the closer reality of God's presence. Moments of God's in-dwelling, which can be called sacramental moments, may indeed take place outside of the church. The sacraments of the church are often not a place where people find this closeness, despite the incorporation of two important elements into a sacramental moment. These elements are: a sense of resonance, which has been described as a thread connecting us to the past and pulling us into the future; and the use of symbols such as water, bread and wine which help open up the imagination. Often, these elements do not work as they should because the thread has been broken and the resonance lost, a loss deepened by the starkness of a Reformed tradition which shies away from the use of symbol.

- *Do you find that any of the sacraments specifically help you to feel part of a moment when God is particularly close?*
- *Have you ever felt a sacramental moment outwith the particular sacraments of the church?*
- *Do you think that there are ways to enrich the experience of sacraments within the church?*

Share your experience and ideas with your group.

LIVING CHRISTIANITY

What does it mean to live as someone who believes in God in modern Scotland? In this unit we will look at how faith and belief in God touches and affects the way in which we live. Does believing in God make a difference? Does believing make it harder to make the choices we face every day?

To start, ask yourself these questions:

- *How does believing in God change my life?*
- *How much are my choices shaped by my beliefs?*
- *What do I have to do to be a Christian?*

Share your first impressions with the group.

One of the literal meanings of the word 'belief' in old German is 'to rest my love in you'. In western understanding, belief is usually about holding to particular intellectual values. But if you believe in something or someone - if you 'rest your love in them' - you have put your trust in them. Belief is about relationship. Being a Christian, and therefore believing in God, is something which affects the way in which you relate to others, to the created world and to yourself. Relationships that will be influenced in this way are to do with:

Myself... ethical choices; what do I think about my body; and how do I use it?

Others... connections with others: what do I feel about the choices other people make and how they affect me? What sort of society should I try to live in? What do I do about people who are 'different' from me?

Creation... the environment and ecology: what can I do in a world which is in crisis? Should I care about God's creation?

Spiritual....how can I apply my religious beliefs sensibly and practically in my day to day life? How do I answer the problems of suffering and evil which are all around me? How free am I at the end of the day?

Ultimate...life after death... is it all pointless? Is there a life beyond death? Does God have a plan for the world and for me?

Relating to myself

One of the things which Scripture makes clear is that the human individual is created in the image of God. From the beginning of their history the Jewish people were aware of and celebrated the particular care and love which God gave to humanity, not least by entering into a relationship with them.

At the time of Jesus there was a common belief, deeply influenced by Greek philosophy, suggesting that the physical human body was merely a vehicle for the spiritual soul to live in. Indeed, some people saw the body as a spirit. Because of this divisive way of looking at the body, many people felt that what was done to the body didn't ultimately matter. All that mattered was looking after one's soul. In turn, it was believed by many that the human soul was in a sense imprisoned in the body as a result of the human birth process - the pain and distress of childbearing God promised Eve after the Fall from Eden, and thus for which woman was believed to be responsible. For that reason the soul was viewed as being masculine, and the body as impure and therefore female. This kind of belief is called dualistic - because it splits things into two.

The New Testament writers, particularly St Paul, argue very strongly against this. Indeed, the 'Incarnation' of Jesus was all about God taking on our human flesh. To answer critics, St Paul argues in 1 Corinthians that what we do and how we use and treat our physical bodies will profoundly affect our spiritual and psychological lives and vice-versa. Paul argues that as we are part of the body of Christ, the way we treat our bodies will influence our relationship with God.

Despite such arguments the early Church, especially in its reaction to women and sexuality, adopted many of the divisive patterns of Greek philosophy noted above. As a result many people engaged in extreme practices in their religious habits, such as denying themselves food and water, in an attempt to subdue their physical needs. These influences can still be seen today. However there is also a significant strand within Scripture which points to the need for Christians to celebrate their bodies as gifts from God. If we are unique and special to God then we become the living image of God. We are called to celebrate that relationship and that involves allowing ourselves to use our body to express that joyful relationship fully.

As a consequence, what we do with our bodies is, for many Christians, caught up in a confused understanding of the relationship between the spiritual and the physical within each of us. Christian tradition has often left people with a sense of guilt or uncertainty about their bodies. On the one hand there is a feeling that the body is a potential source of sin, yet on the other hand we are called to use our bodies to celebrate God.

- *Do you think what you do to/ with your body affects your relationship with God?*
- *Do you see your body as something you do not fully control? Has it a power to tempt you to do things which you do not want to do?*

- *Look at the images of the human body represented here.*
- *How do they convey the human body? Do they value or denigrate the body?*

An issue which many Christians find most difficult is that which has to do with sex; including sexuality, and sexual orientation. Scripture has many, often contradictory, things to say on this subject. Our sexuality is not separate from our spirituality or our physicality. It is part of who we are and what makes us tick. Sexuality in this sense is part of our make-up as created beings, and is therefore a gift from God, a gift allowing for many forms of expression. The sexual act is part of our sexuality but not the whole of it, being necessary for human fulfilment and survival.

As Christians, we are at times very confused about our sexuality and the sexual act, because Christianity has inherited the Greek idea of duality - the split between body and soul. Taking this to its logical conclusion, the body, as represented by the physical and therefore the sexual aspects, has been considered to be potentially evil and dangerous. Society, influenced by this sense of danger, has created rules for the sexual act, which prohibit sex unless some conditions are met. Historically speaking, it has been generally considered most acceptable to have sexual relationships with someone of the opposite gender who is close to you in age, race and social status.

Many people look to Scripture to help them decide what attitudes and values they should hold. This is not always an easy process, particularly in the case of sexual ethics. It is perhaps especially evident in regard to male homosexuality (the Bible is reticent on the subject of lesbianism). Here people often look to the Deuteronomic and Levitical texts to provide an exact and complete answer in a manner quite dissimilar from the way in which they normally use Scripture.

Look at the following texts.

- *Do you read them in the same way?*
- *Has one greater significance than the other? Why?*

> 'No man is to have sexual relations with another man. God hates that.'
>
> Leviticus 18:22

> 'Do not wear clothes made of two kinds of material.'
>
> Leviticus 19:19b

> 'When a woman has her monthly period, she remains unclean for seven days. Anyone who touches her is unclean until evening.'
>
> Leviticus 15:19
>
> Good News Bible

Discuss how you think you should make choices about sexual ethics

- *Should these be taken straight from Scripture*
- *Be influenced by contemporary society, be shaped by what you feel God is telling you*
- *Or a mixture of all of these?*

Relating to others

We all live in relationship to other people, and we rarely make choices which do not touch the lives of those around us. Therefore we wish to hold some of our beliefs not just as personal truths, but as universal, God-given edicts for humanity. In claiming that our truths have a universal application, we often seek to make our belief into law, to ensure that all society is bound by it. Many people nowadays say that fewer truths should be regarded as universal, but rather we should accept a diversity of opinion on many ethical subjects.

There is a tension within Scripture between, on the one hand, the sense that we are all responsible to one another for what we do (I am my brother's keeper) and, on the other, the freedom which God has given each of us. Christian teaching affirms that we all depend on one another, that we are linked or related, in community. What we do, even to ourselves, affects other people. So to some extent we have a responsibility for our personal actions which lies outwith the effect they may have on us. Even an action which seems centred on myself, such as choosing to take my own life, has an impact upon those who know and love me.

- *Do you think that everything you do affects other people?*
- *What restricts you from doing what you want to do - money, law, convention, thinking about others?*
- *Someone once said, 'I should be allowed to do whatever I want to, as long as I don't harm anyone else.' Do you agree?*

While parts of Scripture seem to provide us with absolute statements about what is right and wrong, there are many complex contemporary issues on which the Bible is silent or contradictory. Euthanasia and abortion both raise profound questions about who 'owns' life, and whether a choice which results in death can ever be regarded as either necessary, or as holding within it grace and dignity. Yet Scripture provides us with no absolute indication of what we should feel about these issues.

The Old Testament provides us with many examples, mainly in Leviticus and Deuteronomy, of the legal code under which the people of those times had to live. Through these books and others, notably the prophets, we gain an understanding of God's insistence on a code for a nation, not just for individuals. However, as the Christian ethic has developed, it has been criticised for being too individualistic. It has been accused of concerning itself overly with personal morality while neglecting the demand for a just society, with strong obligations to the weak, marginalised and socially excluded.

Look at the Ten Commandments in Exodus 20:1-17.

- *What do you think each commandment says to society as a whole, not just the individuals within it?*

Relating to creation

Over the last few years, there has been a growing sense of a planet in chaos. Warnings about the destruction of the ozone layer, the increase in global warming and the extinction of species of plants and animals have left many with feelings of fear and guilt. Actions we have taken in the twentieth century, which have increased the standard of living for many in the West, have had terrible repercussions for the global environment, and for people and places in other parts of the world. While individuals often endeavour to help by recycling or using more environmentally friendly products, western governments continue to refuse to make decisions which would have more fundamental and far-reaching consequences.

More recently too, negative side-effects of the ways in which humanity has sought to increase farming production have resulted in scares about public health, with threats found in products ranging from eggs to beef. We are all increasingly aware of the fragile relationships we have with the natural world, especially when challenged with debate about the potential benefits and dangers of animal cloning and genetically modified crops. Such issues raise important questions for the way in which Christians relate to God's world, as inhabitants and co-creators. One of the insights of Genesis is that to an extent we share with God in the continual creation of the world of which we are a part. How we do that affects not only the relationship we have with creation but also our relationship with God.

Look at the following extract:

> There are many points to be said in favour of the potential of genetically modified food, and also some fundamental ethical objections and risk concerns. The environmental advantages of reducing chemical inputs to the land, the possibility of growing crops in hitherto marginal regions of the Third World, and the improvements in nutritional qualities of food are excellent goals, and would be welcomed by most people. Many potential benefits are, however, a long way from reality. By the nature of things, it will be some years before a clear picture emerges of the balance of environmental effects, positive and negative. The science of genetics needs to be met with a comparable understanding of the ecological complexity of the environment into which the modified crops would come. If genetically modified organisms were going to make the difference between people going hungry or having enough to eat, then there would be a clear ethical case for the risks to ecological balance or human health to be worth taking. This case is also a very long way from being proven, however, not least because most of the products currently in prospect do not seem to be meeting any obvious human needs, against which the rhetoric of 'feeding the world' at present seems very hollow.
>
> from the Report of the Board of National Mission to the General Assembly of the Church of Scotland, 1999

Only very recently, human beings have been developing abilities to create and mould life in ways which were thought previously to be in God's power alone - specifically, genetic engineering. The controversy surrounding Dolly the Sheep raised many questions for Christians about our freedom to manipulate and control the most fundamental elements of creation and genesis. The way in which the insights of science have been abused with regard to the natural world has led many people to be concerned that the insights of the new science of genetics will be misused, and may lead to harm rather than benefit. Scientists argue that there is a tremendous potential for research in the alleviation of diseases passed down through genes, such as some cancers, muscular dystrophy and Alzheimer's disease. But others suggest that the cost of interfering with the natural human make-up may not be worth the gain.

- *In which areas do you think we should put a STOP sign up for scientists and researchers?*
- *Why?*

Relating spiritually

One of the most painful struggles that many people go through in their relationship with God is seeking to understand why the world contains so much evil and seemingly unnecessary pain. This question has troubled humanity throughout history; the Old Testament is rich in writings in which men and women attempt to grapple with these points. For example, in the book of Job and in many of the psalms, we see writers trying to reconcile belief in an all-powerful God with the terrible and unfair things which happen to people trying to live a good life.

Look at the following quotes. Which would you say best expresses the way you feel about this issue?

> 'I suppose that God must have some great plan, and in the end we will understand why such awful things are allowed to happen.'
>
> 'It isn't really to do with God when something bad happens. After all we were given the power to make bad decisions as well as good. After that it was up to us.'
>
> 'If we had a world without suffering, we wouldn't really live life to the fullest; because without knowing pain, we would never really know we were happy.'

'Bad things happen for a reason. I think that I have grown stronger through my response to the difficulties I have encountered in life.'

'We don't have the right to try to understand God, or to try to say what is good and what is bad to God. God is so much bigger that we shouldn't think that his notions of good or bad are the same as ours.'

'There is a force in the world, call it the devil if you like, who influences us towards evil.'

'Evil is in the world because we don't try hard enough to live our lives the way God wants us to.'

Share your responses with the group.

Relating ultimately

Most of the time we live each day as it comes, giving little thought to what might be called ultimate questions. Is life pointless? Why are we here? Is there a life beyond death? At critical moments however, usually of crisis and change in our lives, we draw back and take time out from simply existing in order to think about the meaning of life, death and ultimately what relationships are all about.

The Bible gives voice to these questions and many others. In Christian understanding life is precious, but a distinction is drawn between merely getting by or existing, and having a quality of relationship and living which Christ describes as 'fullness'. That which prevents us from living fully is rightly called sin, because it often results in our falling short in our relationship with God. There is much within ordinary living and the existence of our world which limits the fullness which God promises.

Life is created to be enjoyed, to be lived to the full, to be celebrated, cherished and welcomed like a good meal or wine. It is the most precious gift we each of us have, and yet often we can get so obsessed with the minutiae of living that we fail to recognise the rhythm of life. People frequently feel that life is not theirs to control. Whether it be poverty, accident, the loss of someone loved, some events are to a greater or lesser extent beyond our control. One of the New Testament instructions is the command not to worry about tomorrow because tomorrow will provide enough worries of its own (Matthew 6:34). To some degree that makes us concentrate on what we can achieve today, on taking charge of our day-to-day living and challenging all that prevents us and others from possessing and claiming fullness of life.

Christian theology celebrates belief in resurrection. Life is not meaningless but is filled with purpose, a purpose that we cannot always understand and which is not limited to our existence in time. The resurrection of Jesus celebrated the triumph of life. Life does not just relate to itself but continues after death. Our relationship with God continues after death. There is a particular emphasis that there will be a sense of recognition and belonging, a continuance of both our relationship to God and to one another after death. Christ promised that through faith in him and through his resurrection, we have the assurance that life is not just what we see and feel here but something far greater. This promise, which the church has sometimes found difficult to live up to, should make us stop and think: that, rather than seeing our life on earth as less important, this compels us to live that life and value that living to the full.

Here are three attitudes to life and death:

The poet John O'Donohue compares the case of what might happen if two lovers fall out of love with one another and one of them decides to go to the far end of the world. It would still be possible, two or three years down the line, when an aching void is felt, for one of them to get on a plane, fly to the other side of the world, and simply sit and watch their loved one: to see their face again, hear their voice even from a distance. But there is no plane, no journey which can be taken, when someone dies. They are gone. Their face cannot be seen, their voice is silent, their presence a memory. This is the finality of death. But this also shows how precious life is. Each moment, each encounter, each glance holds a uniqueness, a sense of value all its own. Life is for living now because it cannot be repeated, not even a second of it.

Musician Tom Waits once spoke about the specialness of each moment. If after death we were allowed to return even for five minutes, whatever five minutes we were given would become deeply precious to us. Even five minutes spent doing something routine or boring would suddenly become a treasure.

There was once a prisoner who sang a song in a prison one night. He sang 'Home Sweet Home'. It was so moving that that night seven of the prisoners escaped, and the next day were found - in their homes.

Reflect on these three accounts.

- *What do these ideas say to you?*
- *What might be different about your life, if you 'lived life to the fullest'?*
- *What can you do to make your life 'full'?*

Linked to almost all we have said thus far - about relating to ourselves, to others, to creation, relating spiritually and ultimately - is the issue of whether or not God has an overall purpose, plan or pattern for us. We are, in some way, asking the question: how does God relate to us? How does God relate to the dance of life?

- *Does God stand and watch us as we stumble and take the wrong steps?*
- *Is God a partner guiding us gently through the steps?*
- *Is God sometimes involved, but sometimes sitting this one out?*
- *Did God write the steps of the dance which we have to follow exactly?*
- *Is God perhaps the music rather than the dance?*

What do you think?

GOD

Background to the idea of God in the Old Testament

The authors mainly try to explain their understanding of the nature of God through stories, which place God at the centre of a narrative, rather than through a theological discussion. God is presented as the creator and sustainer of the world, who enters into a relationship with the chosen people of Israel - a relationship with promises and obligations on both sides which is called a 'covenant'. By honouring the relationship they are kept in union with God. The language used to describe God was commonplace at the time. Therefore a lot of the images are masculine; king, father, judge, shepherd. However there are also strong female images of mother, midwife and nurse. God is given a number of names in the Hebrew scriptures, the most common is, 'Yahweh' - a holy name which is too special for Jews to say - and Elohim, which means 'Our God'.

Other gods were considered irrelevant (2 Chronicles 2.5) and Yahweh was originally understood to be the only God to be reckoned with. Scattered through the early part of the Old Testament are human expressions for God where he appears as a man: e.g. Genesis 18.1ff and Ezekiel 1:26.

A lot of the understanding of the nature of God we have at present goes back to the period of the Exodus. Here God is seen as having a sacred relationship with the people of Israel. There are commands and legal sanctions and he is the source and sustainer of all power.

The prophets helped to develop the people's understanding of God's character. Amos preached that the righteousness of God was limited by no national boundaries. Hosea was the first to talk of his fatherhood and his mercy. Isaiah wrote about God's holiness and transcendence. Jonah pictured Yahweh as the saviour of the gentiles, or non-Jews, also.

By the time the Hebrew scriptures of the Old Testament had been written and collected together, the understanding of God had changed considerably and there is within the many books a diversity of concepts and understandings of God. That understanding incorporates several key features important to our view of God today - monotheism (only one God exists); that physical representations (idols) of God are outlawed; that Yahweh is seen as the creator of the universe, including human beings, and as the giver of a moral code by which we can live.

Background to the understanding of God in the New Testament

The major difference between the Old Testament and the New is that the world which the writers of the New Testament inhabited is very different from that of the Hebrew writers. Much of the New Testament reflects the fact that the early Christian church was influenced by the thought, philosophy and culture of the Greek and Roman society in which it found itself. The early Christians sought to communicate their 'good news', and to do this effectively they tried to put their ideas, and describe God, in ways which the people of the time could understand. As a result, much of the language and thought which come to us from the older Hebrew scriptures are not found in the New Testament.

For instance, images which were used were of things which people would readily recognise: Paul uses the language of the law-courts to speak of the way in which we are put into a right relationship with God. Philosophical ideas of the time, including the notion of perfection, also began to play a part in Christian thought alongside Hebrew ideas.

Further, belief in God becoming human was a sea-change in the way in which God had been understood up until that time; a radical shift for Christians in that they believe in a God who becomes one of us, living our lives and sharing our experiences.

The way an understanding of God is gained is now not solely through reading about his relationship with a people, as in the Old Testament, but by looking at the person of Jesus Christ. For this reason, the dominant concept used to describe God is 'Abba' (Father). Referring to God as Father is not unique to Christianity - what is different is the way in which God is seen as becoming and being human in the New Testament.

In the New Testament, although there are passages suggesting the unity of Father and Son there are also passages drawing a clear distinction between the two.

God after the New Testament:

In the period of the early Church (the first - fourth centuries C.E.), the doctrine of God developed through: a relationship between the information given in Scripture, the controversies with pagans, Jews and heretics, and Greek philosophy as the foundation of most of the educational processes of those creating the theology of the early church.

By the time of the Council of Nicaea (in 325 C.E. - a major gathering or council of the early church from which the Nicene Creed came), the broad lines of Christian thought were fixed. There was much discussion and debate on the nature of God and of the relationship between Father, Son and Spirit. It was at this time that the doctrine of the Trinity arose. There was also a re-emphasis on God's nature as being eternal, omnipotent (having power over everything), and immutable (not changing).

St. Augustine (354 - 430), one of the greatest of the early church thinkers, said that while we can assert positive things about God, i.e., God is good, we are not saying that God's goodness is equivalent to or the same as human goodness. He advanced philosophical proofs for the existence of God which theologians of the Middle Ages such as St Anselm (1033-1109) were keen to see developed into a systematic and reasoned view of God. Reformers in the 16th century in turn sought to emphasise the personal relationship of God with individual believers.

The Enlightenment, and the renaissance of science through thinkers such as Galileo and Darwin, brought particular challenges to a traditional view of God. There was a profound questioning of the literal truth of the biblical stories, not least of creation. This resulted in major changes in biblical scholarship and in the ways in which theologians spoke of God. There was a cultural emphasis on the role and rights of the individual, and a questioning of moral order and authority which affected the Church's position in society and her ability to take for granted popular belief in God.

In more recent times the understanding of God has been challenged by historical events. The way in which people spoke of God after the horrors of the Holocaust changed for ever. God was re-emphasised not as a detached, distant being but as one who was inextricably linked and involved in the suffering of humanity. The re-emphasis on the environment in recent decades has encouraged theologians to re-discover the scriptural emphasis on God as creator, and humanity's responsibility as part of creation.

One of the critical changes in the understanding of God has been the awareness that the pictures we have of God have been frequently rooted in a particular way of understanding society. This view has often placed God at the top, making the divine support the side of the victors and rulers. Cultures such as those in Latin America, Asia, Africa and India, together with women, ethnic groupings and gay people have increasingly sought to express their relationship with God in ways which speak to them. In Scotland the re-emphasis on Celtic Christianity has in part reflected a desire to speak of God in words, images and stories which relate to the culture and history of the people.

further reading

JESUS

Jesus the Saviour

Over the centuries writers and thinkers have developed different ways of looking at the way in which Jesus saves.

Salvation

Salvation has to do with being saved; but this has meant very different things during the development of the early church and since then.

Historically for the Jews, the idea of salvation was related to the dream of being restored into a proper and right relationship with God. This meant that the covenant between them and God (referred to on **page 30**) would be restored. This had come to imply a political and cultural restoration. For the prophet Isaiah, salvation meant first and foremost, freedom in practice from the Babylonians and a restoration and re-building of the Temple in Jerusalem, the holiest of holies for the Jewish people. For a prophet like Ezekiel, it meant the restoration of justice, and the proper worship of God; which he graphically describes as God himself becoming the shepherd of his flock (the people of Israel) in the place of all the corrupt and weak 'shepherds' which they then had (i.e. the rulers and kings).

> I myself will be the shepherd of my sheep, and I will make them lie down, says the Lord God. I will seek the lost, and I will bring back the strayed, and I will bind up the injured, and I will strengthen the weak, but the fat and the strong I will destroy. I will feed them with justice.
>
> Ezekiel 34:15-16

By the time of Jesus, there had been an increased hope that the Messiah would come and would bring with him release from the powerful rule of the Romans.

Within early Christianity there was the same sense that salvation from God would mean a restoration, a renewal of a true and proper relationship with God. Explicitly for them, it would mean the final defeat of death and the resurrection back to life of all those who had died. There was also a sense in some of the writings of the New Testament that this salvation was already beginning because Jesus Christ had started the kingdom of God by coming to earth, by dying and rising again to life.

Yet as the years rolled on and the promised return of Jesus (known as the *parousia*) did not happen, the early Christians had to start living their lives, still expectant, but nevertheless working out and communicating the story of salvation to others. Salvation in practice, therefore, became much more about discipleship.

Salvation, for Christians in the early church and later, emphasised the central position of Christ on the cross in the defeat of evil, and his transcending the tomb in defeating death and darkness. There is a tremendous amount of literature and art, especially in the middle ages, which concentrates on the Cross, and the saving act of Christ. The death of Jesus on the Cross and what it meant is known as 'atonement' - it is the belief that he takes upon himself the sins of the world so that we might have life. However there are many different ways of understanding what was happening on the Cross and in the tomb. Christians are not in full agreement on these matters. What they do agree is that in some way or other Christ was acting as the one who saves and restores us to relationship with God and with one another.

The Cross as sacrifice

The view of 'the Cross as sacrifice' is strongly influenced by the sacrificial system of the Old Testament. It involved making sacrifices of different kinds but contained at its heart the idea of offering gifts to God in the hope of averting his wrath.

It is hard for us to understand how sacrifices were thought to work but the key element was the idea of purification. Unless one was pure one could not endure being near God. If you look at Hebrews 10:1-14 you can see the way in which this sort of understanding was applied to early Christian views of Jesus.

For the writer of John in particular, the death of Jesus was closely linked to the sacrifice of the lamb in the Temple during the Jewish festival known as Passover, which commemorated the power of death passing over the people of Israel as they fled out of Egypt. Like the Passover lamb Jesus had to be free of blemish, offering himself on behalf of our sins. Jesus through his sacrifice puts us into a restored relationship with God.

The Cross as place of victory

> Since the children, as he calls them, are people of flesh and blood, Jesus himself became like them and shared their human nature. He did this so that through death he might destroy the one who has the power over death, that is, the devil...
>
> Hebrews 2:14.

This is a very ancient view. Some argue that there is a sense in which the Cross represents God's struggle and victory over evil. Those who support this view suggest that the Cross gives evidence of God's defeat over all that is negative in our experience and our world. It is there that sickness, disease, powerlessness, evil and despair all find their defeat. Yet for many examining our own world, the battle seems still to be waging.

The Cross as a place of punishment

> They sing a new song:
> 'You are worthy to take the scroll
> and to open its seals,
> for you were slaughtered and by your
> blood you ransomed for God
> saints from every tribe and
> language and people
> and nation;
> you have made them to be a kingdom
> and priests serving our God,
> and they will reign on earth.'
>
> Revelation 5:9-10.

Humanity is considered to have sinned against the law of God and so, as a result, there needs to be some punishment for this sin. It is because God is just that the law needs to be upheld: Jesus, according to this view, takes the punishment on to himself which is due to us. This is known as the 'substitutionary' theory and has been very popular in Christian belief on salvation. Christ pays the debt which is really ours and therefore we are personally obliged to him for his action. Indeed the accumulation of our sin is so great that it is only Christ who is able to receive the punishment for the sins of humanity. Throughout the history of Christian thought, this has been a very common and much used way of understanding the Cross.

The Cross as a place of love

> Those who believe in him are not condemned; but those who do not believe are condemned already, because they have not believed in the name of the only Son of God.
>
> John 3:18.

further reading

This argues that the Cross is an extravagant demonstration of God's love for us which demands a response of love from us. If God so loved the world that Christ died for us we can do no other but respond in love by repenting for all that we have done wrongly. If someone does something very generous for us, we might respond in kind and do something which we had not intended doing until witnessing that gesture of love. This theory argues that the Cross influences us to change our way of behaving morally.

The Cross as a place of God's suffering

This view is relatively recent: it shows how people have changed their ideas on what happened on the Cross, and indeed what salvation is. After some of the horrendous horrors of the 20th century, particularly the Holocaust, it became clear for many that it would no longer be possible to speak of God saving the world in language which seemed to be simplistic and ignored the suffering of the world. This view claims that God deals with human failure by his presence in its consequences, through which the failure is redeemed. God is the God who was present in the concentration camps as Jews, homosexuals, gypsies and the disabled were murdered. The crucifixion of Jesus is but the most vivid demonstration of what is always true, that God suffers with the suffering of his world, and is able to forgive because he has the right of the victim to forgive. God's forgiveness does not come cheaply: he is not a bystander forgiving a sin whose consequences were suffered by others, for he was there, enduring with those who suffer.

More recently there has been a stress placed on salvation as leading to political and social justice. The influence of theologies from the developing world have underlined and reminded Christians of the way in which to be saved by God means to be restored to just and right relationships with one another and with the created world. There is also a sense in which salvation offers spiritual freedom, gives us a sense of spiritual well-being, re-orders our priorities in living and gives purpose to our existence.

Quick thoughts on some of the terms for Jesus:

The Messiah

- One of the terms used for the Messiah is the Christ which strictly means 'anointed one', and has a long and rich history of usage and meaning in Jewish understanding.
- Its early use applied to kings in David's line:

Great triumphs he gives to his king,
and shows steadfast love to his anointed,
to David and his descendants for ever.

Psalm 18:50

- It is associated with the expectation that God would raise up an ideal ruler to the throne of David.

In those days and at that time I will cause a righteous Branch to spring up for David; and he shall execute justice and righteousness in the land.

Jeremiah 33:15

- The word could also apply to anyone given a divine task that affected the people of Israel.

Thus says the Lord to his anointed, to Cyrus,
whose right hand I have grasped
to subdue nations before him
and strip kings of their robes,
to open doors before him -
and the gates shall not be closed.

Isaiah 45:1

- Jesus seemed to be reluctant to accept the title Messiah without qualification:

And he sternly ordered them not to tell anyone about him.
Then he began to teach them that the Son of Man must undergo great suffering, and be rejected by the elders, the chief priests, and the scribes, and be killed, and after three days rise again.

Mark. 8:30-31

- Passages frequently refer to Jesus 'who was called the Christ'

Pilate said to them, 'Then what should I do with Jesus who is called the Messiah?' All of them said 'Let him be crucified!'

Matthew 27:22

This may represent an early tradition that Jesus was called Messiah by others.

- John says explicitly that such a title should not be seen politically

> Jesus answered, 'My kingdom is not from this world. If my kingdom were from this world, my followers would be fighting to keep me from being handed over to the Jews. But as it is, my kingdom is not from here.' Pilate asked him, 'So you are a king?' Jesus answered, 'You say that I am a king. For this I was born, and for this I came into the world, to testify to the truth. Everyone who belongs to the truth listens to my voice.
>
> John 18:36-37

- Jesus arouses the expectation that he is appointed by God through such events as the entry into Jerusalem and the cleansing of the Temple, both episodes having been spoken of as the fulfilment of previous prophecies.

- After Jesus' death and resurrection Christians applied the title of 'Messiah' to Jesus - Jesus becomes the agent crucified for our sins and becomes linked to the theme of the 'suffering servant' in Isaiah; e.g. 52:13ff.

> For I handed on to you as of first importance what I in turn had received: that Christ died for our sins in accordance with the scriptures...
>
> 1 Cor 15:3

Also,

> Was it not necessary that the Messiah should suffer these things and then enter into his glory?' ...
> ...and he said to them, 'Thus it is written, that the Messiah is to suffer and to rise from the dead on the third day.
>
> Luke 24:26, 46.

- In the New Testament 'Christ' is also used as part of Jesus' name.

> Let it be known to all of you, and to all the people of Israel, that this man is standing before you in good health by the name of Jesus Christ of Nazareth, whom you crucified, whom God raised from the dead.
>
> Acts 4:10

- The term 'messiah' tended to drop from Christian usage in the historical period after the early Church because the people who were awaiting a Messiah in their own lives and experience were now no more.

- There is an important link today to the Jewish origins of the term Messiah - many Jews who convert to Christianity today are often termed as Messianic Jews, because they consider themselves Jews who have accepted the Messiahship of Christ.

Son of God

- Jesus accepts it:

> Again the high priest asked him, 'Are you the Messiah, the Son of the Blessed One?' Jesus said. 'I am; and "you will see the Son of Man seated at the right hand of the Power", and "coming with the clouds of heaven." '
>
> Mark 14:61-62

- John's use of the term 'Son of God' for Christ, and the term 'children' for believers, is suggestive of the relationship between believers and God. Although scholars debate the authenticity of passages where Jesus calls himself the Son of God, (i.e. John 11:4), the early Church used the term to underline the divinity of Jesus. The early Church also wanted to make sure that people understood the difference between Christ and God - the term 'son' allowed them to do this. Today there might be problems with this term in that it may suggest an inequality in the relationship between Jesus and God, for Christian teaching affirms that Jesus and God the Father are equal.

Jesus as Lord

- The early Jewish historian Josephus records the information that one of the reasons which the Jews refused to take part in the worship of the Roman emperor cult was because they would have had to call him Lord. For the Jews the term was already closely linked to Yahweh. So when Christians began to use the term and to link it closely with Jesus, it carried with it a particular focus and force.

- There are lots of New Testament passages which use Hebrew passages as explicit references to Christ.

> So that at the name of Jesus, every knee should bend, in heaven and on earth and under the earth, and every tongue should confess that Jesus Christ is Lord, to the glory of God the Father.
>
> Philippians 2:10-11

- This takes the declaration from Isaiah 45:23 'every knee':

> By myself I have sworn,
> from my mouth has gone forth in righteousness
> a word that shall not return:
> To me every knee shall bow,
> every tongue shall swear.

- The term 'lord' became very popular in the middle ages. These were feudal times and the lords or local princes held considerable power over those under their authority. One has to remember the extremely hierarchical nature of society with the king (ruling absolutely) at the top, a hierarchy down through lesser nobles and servants, and with serfs at the bottom of the ladder. These cultural associations were easily transferred to ideas about the church. So God is seen as the King, Jesus as the Lord and the people come way down at the bottom.

- In our own culture the use of the word 'lord' is somewhat mixed. It is not often used and when it is it may still be a term with negative hierarchical connotations, e.g., the House of Lords, traditional land-owners and so on.

Jesus the Word

- *Logos* means 'word' or 'reason' to the Greeks, and the two meanings are always intertwined. *Logos* puts the sense into the word.

- In Jewish thought, 'the Word' is not just what things are called, it also performs an action.

- A Jewish philosopher called Philo a few decades before Jesus had tried to blend together Jewish and Greek thought by saying that the *logos* is 'the tiller by which the pilot of the universe steers all things.' It is the bridge between God and humanity.

- John is doing something extraordinary, not dreamt of by Philo, in saying that the *logos* had become flesh.

- John was doing some very significant things:

  - He was clothing Jesus in language that some of the non-Jewish world could understand, by using a term familiar to the Greeks.
  - He was saying that Jesus is the creating power of God, the divine spark, come to us. He does not only speak the Word of knowledge; he speaks the Word of power.
  - He was saying that Jesus is the incarnate mind of God. A word is always the expression of a thought and Jesus is the perfect expression of God's thought for humanity.

- The term 'Word' became very significant in the early Church. There was a great emphasis on it and its associated Greek thought, in order to stress that Jesus the Word had been with God at the beginning of the world, and so was with God for all eternity.

- The reformers in the 15th century stressed both the theology and practice of the Word too. But there was also at that time the start of a popular confusion between speaking of 'the Word' as Jesus and the Word of God as Scripture.

THE BIBLE

Israel's beginnings and the Laws

- The first five books of the Old Testament, also called the Pentateuch, are the foundation-documents for the people of Israel.
- Ancient tradition said that they had all been written by Moses, since he was regarded as the architect of Israel as a country in its own right; but they were not in fact written by a single person.
- These books were formed gradually over a period of six hundred years, from earlier oral stories and collections of writings, gradually changed, developed and brought together into the final form that we now have.
- Sometimes, different versions of the same story - like the two quite different creation-stories in Genesis 1 and 2 - were allowed to sit side by side, with no attempt at integration.
- The process of putting this together was all going on during the period in which Israel was coming to an awareness of itself as a nation; and the way the books have come together reflects this.
- The Exodus from Egypt was a key event, and was very important in forming Israel's identity as a nation.
- The books also reflect developments in the Hebrew religion, ending up with the worship of one God; as opposed to the worship of many gods which was part of the earliest Hebrew tradition.

The history of Israel

- Joshua, Judges, 1 Samuel, 2 Samuel, 1 Kings and 2 Kings make up in effect a single historical narrative, though one which has used a variety of sources.
- These sources included legends and stories from separate geographical sites which had become part of the background of each of the different shrines where worship took place.
- Some of the oldest parts of the Bible (in terms of their composition) are in the book of Judges - which was written more than three thousand years ago.
- The historical books, which have been edited and re-edited a number of times, were not put together for the sake of relating history. They were written to make a theological point rather than to offer a description of Israel's history.

The theology of these books is that:

- Israel has been chosen by Yahweh to be his people, and has entered a covenant with God to serve him, and him alone.
- serving God means fulfilling the Law
- the king becomes the focus of the national covenant with Yahweh in later biblical tradition.
- kings who support the worship of Yahweh alone flourish, and with their rule the nation prospers; while kings who allow other religions quickly come to a bad end.
- those who do right are rewarded; those who do not, perish.

The difficulty is that historical facts do not always support the theology, so a fuller interpretation was required.

Poetry and everyday wisdom

- Much of the poetic tradition in wisdom literature comes from the same period as the Deuteronomic history, but its concerns and background are entirely different.
- It is often based on popular wisdom expressed in the 'folk' sayings and dictums of the time.
- It is not concerned much with religious matters like law, salvation or national identity.
- It is concerned most with the practical business of how to live well and wisely in an ordinary, settled life.
- There are examples of wisdom-literature in the Old Testament (Job, Ecclesiastes and Proverbs), and more in the Apocrypha (Wisdom and Ecclesiasticus).
- It is similar in style to literature from other cultures in the ancient east; for instance contemporary Mesopotamian and Egyptian writings.
- Some of the material - for instance Ecclesiastes and some of the psalms - is composed in a form designed to be remembered, and probably taught to children as part of their education.

God certainly features in the Wisdom books, but they mostly don't put forward any particular theology of God. The exception is Job, where a traditional view (shared by the Deuteronomic writers), that God rewards good living and punishes bad, is tackled head-on; but even Job ultimately suggests that it is pointless puzzling over big questions about what God is doing in history, for they are unanswerable. The wise person accepts God's universe, and lives well and faithfully within it.

The Prophets

- This section covers a very long period in history beginning around 800 B.C.E.
- It deals with times that lead up to the exile in Babylon, the return from exile in c. 580 B.C.E., the rebuilding of the Temple at Jerusalem and up to just before the birth of Christ.
- The books of the Prophets were written from the viewpoint of the priests; they tell much of the history of those times from that angle, and deal with the relationship between God and his chosen people in some considerable depth.
- Often they stand in judgement: warning of what will happen if people fail to keep their side of the covenant with God.
- They warn the people about their falling standards in religious observance, their foolish international politics, and their corruption of justice.
- The prophets give priority to justice and integrity, regarding the religious observance of those who exploited others as a sham.
- The nations they attack are prosperous, and beginning to develop 'modern' economies based on large landholding and trade, rather than subsistence-farming. The rich were getting richer and the poor poorer, the prophets deplored this and pointed out the spiritual lesson to be learned.

The Gospels

- The names Mark, Matthew, Luke and John are used by tradition for the writers of the Gospels; but we don't actually know for certain who were the writers.
- They are not attempts to write a biography of Jesus, but are works of theology, written to try to give to the reader a particular understanding of what God was doing through Jesus of Nazareth.
- Matthew, Mark and Luke are closely related works, having a great deal of material in common, and are often called the Synoptic Gospels.
- Mark is the earliest Gospel. He wrote sometime in the 60s C.E, before the fall of the Temple at Jerusalem, and his sources are probably word-of-mouth rather than written material.
- Matthew and Luke wrote at the same time, probably in the years after the fall of Jerusalem; and probably used Mark's writings to help them.
- Luke makes his Gospel the first half of a two-part work, the second part of which continues the story into the times of the early church. We call it the Acts of the Apostles, or just Acts.

further reading

- John's Gospel is not like the other Gospels. It seems to come from later on, and was probably written around the end of the first century C.E. The writer seems to know many of the stories from the synoptic Gospels, and probably had access to them, as well as being in touch with other stories not known to them.

The letters

- Most of the letters in the New Testament are credited to Paul's authorship, and are the oldest documents in the New Testament - they were written several years earlier than any of the Gospels. This means that when Paul tells us of events in Jesus' life (like the account of the Last Supper in 1 Corinthians), it is actually a much older account than any that we have in the Gospels.
- Most were written to particular churches to deal with specific situations or questions which had arisen within these communities.
- A number of the other letters included in the New Testament are not by Paul (for instance Ephesians and Hebrews), and although there is debate about who wrote them, they show something about the issues that were concerning the early church.
- The letters of John may or may not be by the same person as the Gospel of John, but their theology is similar.
- The letter to the Romans is a little different from the others, because it was written to introduce Paul to a church which he had not previously visited. So, acting as an introduction, it is a careful statement of his theology, rather than a response to actual questions and issues. As such, it helps us to see what were the crucial questions to which theology in the early church had to address itself: issues like the relationship of Jew and Gentile, the role of the Law, and christian living in the Roman Empire. Paul's writing style and theology are influenced by his training as a Pharisee (for despite the conflict between Jesus and the Pharisees, Jesus' teaching was far closer to theirs than to any other group).

Revelation

- Revelation is unlike any other New Testament book, though it does have similarities with Daniel and with a whole group of Jewish books circulating about the time of Christ, which were called 'apocalyptic' because they related to the apocalypse, or vision of the day of judgement.
- This is not necessarily a book prophesying the future - it is talking about God's judgement on the present-day situation in John's time.

further reading

- It was written as a result of a vision, to encourage Christians suffering persecution, by 'drawing back the veil of heaven' to show them what is really happening on the cosmic scale. They may see only persecution, but, in heaven, the preparations are already made for their victory.
- It also offers a visual image for every Christian's dream - the coming of the kingdom of God on earth - in its picture of the new Jerusalem.

further reading

WORSHIP

History of worship

Worship as we experience it today in a 'typical' Sunday church service has gone through very many different changes across the centuries. It is not possible to describe them all here but we shall attempt to illustrate some of the major influences.

Christian worship, like so much about the Christian faith, has been greatly influenced by Jewish practices. The story of God's relationship with the people of Israel is full of details about the times, places, people and procedures involved in the true worship of the Lord God. The whole of Jewish life focuses around the Temple, the centre point of worship.

The misdirection of worship into idolatry was a constant theme of the Old Testament. The writers warn against worshipping idols which represented sexuality, political power, false religiosity and sheer selfishness. The prophets in particular harangued people who thought they were doing God's will by attending worship, but were merely going through the motions while not looking after the poor and needy. In other words, from an early stage worship wasn't just about what people did in the Temple (or church) but what they did in the world and the way in which they treated other people.

> I hate, I despise your festivals, and I take no delight in your solemn assemblies. Even though you offer me your burnt offerings and grain offerings I will not accept them; and the offerings of your well fatted animals I will not look upon. Take away from me the noise of your songs; I will not listen to the melody of your harps. But let justice roll down like waters, and righteousness like an ever flowing stream.
>
> Amos 5:21-24

The first thing to note when we look at the New Testament is that it says remarkably little about the worship of the early Christians. This may be for a number of reasons. One is that this was taken for granted - why comment on something so natural and instinctive? The other reason may be that it is clear from early evidence that there was a great variety in forms and patterns of worship and it was only as things became more standardised that these began to be recorded.

Jesus, like the early disciples, worshipped in the synagogue. There he would have experienced prayers and a reading of the scriptures followed by a short address on their meaning. There would also have been a collection of money for the poor in the area, as well as time for singing psalms to God.

Christian worship had at its heart the celebration of Jesus' resurrection. For this reason, the day after the Jewish Sabbath (Saturday) was chosen as the day for the main Christian worship ceremony, because it was the day on which Christ was raised from the dead. Sunday became a day of celebration in which the emphasis was placed on sharing a common meal which remembered Jesus. This meal became known as the *eucharist*, from the Greek word which means 'thanksgiving'. For that reason, worshippers were encouraged to come after having 'confessed' what they had done wrong, where they had sinned. This was to encourage people attending to put themselves back into a right relationship with those they might have wronged before they ate the bread and drank the wine.

In other ways, the early church adapted the mode of worship from Jewish synagogue practice. Prayers were offered to God to give thanks for all the ways in which God had been present in the lives of the community. God was asked to continue to be present and to assist where there were problems. Again, money was shared and given to the poor. A reading was offered, initially from the Old Testament, but gradually from some of the letters and gospels which were being written, which would eventually come together as the New Testament. The short address remained and became what we know today as the sermon.

But before long (within the first generation or two after Christ), the rift between Christians and orthodox Jews led to Christians ceasing to use the Temple and withdrawing from the orthodox synagogues. In some places, Christian synagogues were formed. In others, especially those where there were many non-Jewish believers, the synagogue worship was combined with the breaking of bread in a house-service. This produced a pattern of worship which began with the synagogue style of service - a brief prayer, Bible-readings, sermon and prayers - and continued with the Supper in which there was the taking of bread and wine, giving thanks, and breaking and sharing it. The bread and wine at that point were taken as part of a full supper, though the evidence from the Letter to the Corinthians is that this custom became abused; so, for the sake of conformity of practice, it seems the church soon abandoned a proper meal in favour of using simply bread and wine as a ceremonial meal, as we do today (1 Corinthians 11:20-22). This was the regular pattern on the Lord's Day. Christian hymns soon began to appear, in a style similar to the psalms (Ephesians 5:14 is probably a quotation from such a hymn, as is Philippians 2:6-11).

If the elements of worship were fairly fixed, the style was very free. No one person led the worship. Every believer was originally free to speak, to pray, to prophesy, to lead in a hymn; though some authorities emphasised that this freedom should be restricted to male believers (1 Corinthians 14:26-40).

We also discover in the New Testament that Jesus held both worship and work - his service to God in the Temple and in the World - in very close relationship to one another. So we find him starting his ministry in the synagogue, at times of crisis praying to God, and sharing gifts of bread and wine in a common act of worship in the Upper Room. We read in the Acts of the Apostles of the intimacy which was present in the earliest Christian worship as the first disciples gathered to eat, share and worship God. Worshipping together was a demonstration of what it meant to be a community following Jesus:

> Day by day, as they spent much time together in the temple, they broke bread at home and ate their food with glad and generous hearts, praising God and having the goodwill of all the people.
>
> Acts 2:46-47a

Yet not everyone was agreed on the mechanics of worship. Paul often writes to churches where bad practice (as he saw it) had started to affect their worship; whether this was disorderly behaviour at the meal before the breaking of bread, or women speaking out of turn in the ceremony!

Over the years worship became much more formalised and structured. The practice of having a meal alongside the eucharist was ended. The prayers became more formal. Fewer people took an active part in the conduct of worship, which increasingly became the preserve of the ordained priests and their helpers. The language changed and the church gradually adopted the language of the Roman Empire for all its services. This meant that those who spoke Latin could share the same service in Britain as in Italy. However, the churches in the East continued to use local languages such as Greek, and later Russian, and developed their own elaborate liturgies.

By the middle ages, worship had become formalised to such an extent that the people who attended might have felt that they were watching a performance or a play. The singing was now largely the responsibility of trained choirs. The priest conducted much of the service with his back to the people and spoke in Latin which had long since died out as an everyday language for most people. For many ordinary folk, the elaborate paintings and pictures in their churches were used as visual depictors of the story of God and Jesus.

At the time of the Reformation during the 1500s, there was an attempt to return to a greater sense of involvement by all people in the act of worship. The services were still conducted by a few trained and educated ministers, but the people were encouraged to be involved, not least through the singing of hymns. The use of Latin disappeared and worshippers heard the Gospel in their own languages. If they could, they were encouraged to read the Bible in those languages as well. Yet worship remained for the most part fairly formal, although there was greater spontaneity on the part of the leader. There continued to be a stress on weekly communions, with Reformers like John Knox encouraging this practice, although it did not happen in reality within Scotland.

further reading

It is in the 20th century that the most major changes have taken place in Scottish worship. The end of the 19th century witnessed the introduction of organs into churches and so the practice of unaccompanied singing, often of the psalms, was gradually replaced by Victorian hymns set to the organ. The expansion of ecumenical scholarship in worship and a growing awareness of the practices of other denominations have encouraged a greater variety of worship styles. Church leaders have become increasingly aware of the need to cater for different tastes and temperaments in worship. Hymns have started using modern language and images; music has begun to reflect the popular culture of the time and greater participation in the actual service is given to members of the congregation. Worshippers have been increasingly involved in responsive prayers, in being drawn into the use of images and symbols, in playing a part in dramas and children's talks. Yet in still too many contexts the worshippers remain passive viewers rather than active participants.

SACRAMENTS

Statement of Faith

We believe in one God: Father, Son and Holy Spirit.
God is love.

We praise God the Father:
Who created the universe and keeps it in being.
He has made us his sons and daughters to share his joy,
Living together in justice and peace,
Caring for his world and for each other.

We proclaim Jesus Christ, God the Son:
Born of Mary, by the power of the Holy Spirit,
He became one of us, sharing our life and our death.
He made known God's compassion and mercy,
Giving hope and declaring forgiveness of sin,
Offering healing and wholeness to all.
By his death on the cross and by his resurrection
He has triumphed over evil.
Jesus is Lord of life and of all creation.

We trust God the Holy Spirit:
Who unites us to Christ and gives life to the church;
Who brings us to repentance and assures us of forgiveness.
The Spirit guides us in our understanding of the Bible,
Renews us in the sacraments,
And calls us to serve God in the world.

We rejoice in the gift of eternal life:
We have sure and certain hope of resurrection through Christ,
And we look for his coming again to judge the world.
Then all things will be made new;
And creation will rejoice in worshipping the Father,
through the Son, in the power of the Spirit,
one God, blessed for ever.

Amen

Book of Common Order of the Church of Scotland

The Apostles' Creed

I believe in one God, the Father almighty,
creator of heaven and earth.

I believe in Jesus Christ,
God's only Son, our Lord,
who was conceived by the Holy Spirit,
born of the Virgin Mary,
suffered under Pontius Pilate,
was crucified, died, and was buried;
he descended to the dead.
On the third day he rose again;
he ascended into heaven,
he is seated
at the right hand of the Father,
and he will come to judge
the living and the dead.

I believe in the Holy Spirit,
the holy catholic Church,
the communion of Saints,
the forgiveness of sins,
the resurrection of the body,
and the life everlasting.

Amen

Book of Common Order of the Church of Scotland

Public Profession of Faith

Earlier in the service the minister, recalling the baptism, says:
Do you believe the Christian faith into which we are baptised?
The candidates say together:
I do.
The minister then invites the congregation to stand and with the candidates to affirm the faith in the words of the Apostles' Creed or other statement of faith.

After the prayer for confirmation, the minister says:
You have professed with us your faith in one God, Father, Son and Holy Spirit.
In your baptism God brought you into the house of faith, and in goodness and mercy has shepherded you to this day.
We ask you now to pledge yourself to a life of Christian discipleship:
Do you promise to follow Jesus Christ in your daily life?

Response:
With God's help
I will seek to follow Christ,
And in listening for God's Word,
In the breaking of bread, and prayer,
To grow ever closer to him as the years pass.

Minister:
Do you promise to be a faithful member of the Christian Community?

Response:
With God's help
I will share in the worship and service of the church,
And in this I will give generously
Of what I am and what I have.

Minister:
Do you promise to take part in God's mission to the world?

Response:
With God's help
I will witness to Christ
Wherever I find myself
And putting my trust and hope in him
I will seek justice and peace
And the renewing of all according to God's promise.

The minister may then ask the congregation to respond in the following terms:

Minister
I charge you,
The people of this congregation, to love, encourage and support
These our brothers and sisters in faith,
That they may continue to grow
In the grace of the Lord Jesus Christ
And the knowledge and love of God.

The congregation responds:
With God's help
We will live out our baptism
As a loving community in Christ:
Upholding one another in prayer,
And encouraging one another in service.

from *'Vows of Church Membership'* by the Panel on Worship

References

God

Page 10: 'God the Omnipotent!' by Henry Fothergill Chorley and John Ellerton, from *The Church Hymnary* (3rd Edition), No 516; Oxford University Press 1973, 1975.

Page 11: 'God, our Mother' - authors' original.

Jesus

Page 18: 'There is a green hill far away' by Cecil Francis Alexander, from *The Church Hymnary* (3rd Edition), No 241; Oxford University Press 1973, 1975.

Spirit

Page 27-8: 'In the beginning, God made laughter', source unknown; in *Flowing Streams*, ed. Donald Hilton, NCEC 1993, p. 23.

Page 29: God's Grandeur by Gerard Manley Hopkins, first published (posthumously) by Robert Bridges, 1918, quoted here from *Liturgy of Life,* ed. Donald Hilton; NCEC 1991, p.42.

Page 31: 'She sits like a bird, brooding on the waters' from *Enemy of Apathy*, No. 114; John L Bell and Graham Maule, Wild Goose Publications, 1988.

Page 33: 'The day of Pentecost' by Jenny Mabbott; in *Flowing Streams*, ed. Donald Hilton, NCEC 1993, p. 127.

Prayer

Page 72: extract from *An Evil Cradling* by Brian Keenan; Hutchinson 1992, p.68-69.

Church and Ministry

Page 82: 'This is the mission entrusted to the church'; from *The Violence of Love* by Oscar Romero ISBN 1-800-521-8011 Plough Publishing House, Robertsbridge TN32 5DR (tel. 00 44 1580 88 33 44) pp 29-30.

Worship:

Page 105-6: extract from *The Wind in the Willows* by Kenneth Grahame, first published 1908.

Page 114: Michael Taylor, extracted in *Liturgy of Life,* ed. Donald Hilton, NCEC 1991, p. 161.

Sacraments and other services

Page 121: Baptism service from *Book of Common Order of the Church of Scotland,* St Andrew Press 1994, pp. 86-7, 89.

Page 124: extract from *A Guide to the Sacrament,* John Macquarrie, SCM Press 1997, p.101.

Page 125: 'Bread, wine and gentleness', Anon; in *Flowing Streams,* ed. Donald Hilton, NCEC 1993, p. 111.

Page 128-29: extracts from *Daring to Speak Love's Name: a Gay and Lesbian Prayer Book* edited by Dr Elizabeth Stuart; Hamish Hamilton 1992, p.38-9.

Page 165-66: Statement of Faith and Apostles Creed from *Book of Common Order of the Church of Scotland,* St Andrew Press 1994, endpapers.

Page 166-68: from 'Vows of Church Membership' by the Panel on Worship of the Church of Scotland; Reports to the General Assembly of the Church of Scotland 1996 (25/23) and *Baptisms and Confirmation: their Meaning for the Church* (forthcoming).

Living Christianity

Page 139: Extracted from the report of the Board of National Mission to the General Assembly of the Church of Scotland in 1999; Appendix I, 'The Science and Religion and Technology Report on Genetically Modified Food'; *Reports to the General Assembly,* St Andrew Press 1999, p. 20/103.